Letters to

Letters to Pauline

Stendhal

Translated by Andrew Brown

Hesperus Classics

Hesperus Classics
Published by Hesperus Press Limited
19 Bulstrode Street, London W1U 2JN
www.hesperuspress.com

First published in French in *Lettres intimes*, 1892; *Lettres à Pauline*, 1921;
and *Oeuvres complètes*, 1927–37.
This selection and translation first published by Hesperus Press Limited, 2011

Introduction, selection and English language translation © Andrew Brown, 2011
Foreword © Adam Thirlwell, 2011

Designed and typeset by Fraser Muggeridge studio
Printed in Jordan by Jordan National Press

ISBN: 978-1-84391-167-8

CONTENTS

1

Henri-Marie Beyle, one of whose many pseudonyms was Stendhal, was born in Grenoble, in 1783. Three years later, his sister Pauline was born. When Stendhal was seven, and Pauline was four, their mother died – leaving them to be looked after by their father, whom Stendhal detested; and their maternal grandfather, Gagnon, whom Stendhal adored. Many years later, in 1837, Stendhal decided to sketch a premature obituary, describing how he 'conceived a horror for Grenoble which lasted until his death… His father said to him that he did not want him to lose his morals and that he would not see Paris until he was 30.' His grandfather, however, encouraged Stendhal to learn mathematics, and it was mathematics which allowed Stendhal to leave Grenoble for Paris, when he was sixteen – in 1799 – to study. But he did not study for long. Instead, he began a career in Napoleon's army, and subsequently in the imperial household – a career which would see Stendhal live in Italy, Germany and Russia, as well as Paris, until 1820, when his literary career began in earnest, with the publication of his essay *On Love*. Ten years later, he published his first novel, *The Red and the Black*: the next novel he published was *The Charterhouse of Parma*, in 1839. In 1842, Stendhal died.

So his letters to Pauline, from 1800 to 1825, display a Stendhal who was not yet Stendhal: they mark his effort to become Stendhal. They are memoirs from a time of immaturity. In these letters replete with discarded pseudonyms, letters in which he gives his beloved younger sister advice on how to handle her friends and father, when to marry, what to read, Stendhal therefore has more than one motivation:

    A) Fraternal love for Pauline
    B) Filial hatred of the Family
    C) Egoistic love of Stendhal
    D) Dissident hatred of the Provincial

They try to educate Pauline, but they are also attempts to educate himself. They sketch an imposed escape route for Pauline – the same escape route from the provincial and the family which Stendhal was plotting on his own. Gradually, therefore, a narrative emerges (these letters form an inadvertent epistolary novel): Stendhal – nervy, self-conscious, on the make; and Pauline, stranded in Grenoble, stubborn, wilful, unmarriageable, cool.

Everything, in the end, for both of them, comes down to 'the hunt for happiness'.

How do you think for yourself? This is the paradox which Stendhal was engaged on – in the freestyle novels which made him famous, and in these letters which try to impose freedom on someone else. How do you move away from the mechanics of your family, and find happiness?

2

In these letters, the reader can find Stendhal working out his vocabulary: as he learns to abandon the *melancholy*, and love the *dry*; as he defines the *ridiculous*, and *finesse*. For Stendhal believed in the self-creation of the self. 'Education alone makes men great', he told Pauline; 'consequently, if you wish to become a great genius, you can be one.' These letters to his sister offer a grand rebuke to heredity. They are a form of samizdat – intent on undermining his father's educational régime on Pauline, and replacing it with the free play of Stendhal's reading list: like the libertine novelist Duclos, the enlightenment theorist Montesquieu, or the *Logic* of Tracy. All of them teach a practical philosophy: '*examining*, with the greatest possible precision, the *circumstances of the facts*.' Stendhal's new self – whether male or female – is a new social entity: a bourgeois aristocrat, whose precise pleasures are beyond the bourgeois masses, the snobbish philistines.

Yes, the self, for Stendhal, is a construction: a weird amalgam of the artificial and the natural. And so the reader will discover him placing emphasis on doodled diagrams, or dates – like 16th October 1806 (the day he left Paris for Germany, beginning his career in the imperial administration); or 1804 (when he lived in Paris, trying to be authentically romantic, and make it as a playwright). For a self, and its moral life, is historical, and geographical: even though we so often believe in the timelessness of the emotions, their eternity. The self is datable.

And this is Stendhal's great contribution to literature – here in its most tender, rawest form: the performative self. This was what the French critic Paul Valéry so admired in Stendhal: 'to give people, just by unbuttoning oneself, the sensation of discovering America…': his technique of indecent exposure. 'Literary Egotism', wrote Valéry, 'finally consists in playing *the role of oneself*; to make oneself a little more *natural* than is natural…'

3

The pleasure of Stendhal is in his complicated frankness: his theatrically natural prose. And this requires a similarly frank effort on the part of the reader. There is the danger of being scandalised, or stendhalised ('once again you're going to be stendhalised', he writes in his autobiography.) Stendhal's idea of style places the reader in the distance of the future. The future becomes his metaphor for the necessary distance between author and reader, a theory of the premature which was doodled in a diary entry of 1804: 'I could write a work which I'd be the only person to appreciate and which would be recognised as beautiful in 2000.' But even now, his style requires the reader to match Stendhal's own insouciance.

It is a style full of stops and starts, dense with detail: oblivious to propriety. In 1812, he reported back to Pauline from a burning Moscow, which he had witnessed as a diplomat with Napoleon's army. There is no panache in the sketched description he jotted down for her: instead, the vegetal proliferation of the everyday: 'violent attacks of diarrhoea meant that everyone was worried about the lack of wine.' His prose is a report from the other side of grandeur; the mundane effort of empire. ('I'm glad you have seen war,' he wrote to Pauline two years later, flatly. 'It's interesting.')

This, after all, was the finale of the premature obituary, which he wrote five years before he died, in Paris: 'He respected only one man: NAPOLEON.' And what else was Napoleon but the ultimate self-made man? What else was Napoleon but a miniature Stendhal?

– Adam Thirlwell, 2011

'We who have the inestimable happiness of being passionate', Stendhal writes to his younger sister Pauline on 8th August 1804: the words sound like a rallying cry. And by 'passionate', Stendhal had in mind passions other than the 'vanity' and 'love of money' that in his view drove most of his contemporaries. Passion is often the protest of youth against age, and most of Stendhal's letters to Pauline are the product of youth: at the time of the first of these letters, Stendhal is seventeen and Pauline fifteen. But not all of the passions we find in these letters are the ones we might expect from such young people. First and foremost (and always) comes the passion, simply, for reading and writing – the letters exchanged between brother and sister, of course, but also the *Logique* of Destutt de Tracy, Plutarch's *Lives*, and the plays of 'Chéquspire'. If we imagine Stendhal as leading his life to the accompaniment of popping champagne corks (high society) mixed with the roar of cannon fire and the neighing of horses (his periods soldiering on Napoleon's campaigns in Italy and Russia), embellished with the occasional Mozart or Cimarosa aria sung by a pretty soprano (his love of music, and art, and pretty women too), we are not far wrong: but he was also one of the best-read of novelists, whose curious and inquiring mind led him from a very early age to explore, in several languages, the oddest corners of the literary, historical and philosophical heritage.

The letters begin with what will be a constant complaint: Pauline does not write often enough. He has just moved to Paris, and the first letter acknowledges that he has gone for 'five whole months' without writing to her – but he, if not she, is soon making up for lost time. He wants to read her letters, and he also wants her to read the same books that he reads. She is a willing student in this correspondence course, in which he teaches her all the things he is still learning himself. She keeps us with his discoveries (Shakespeare, Ossian, the latest 'Idéologue' philosophers), but never quite feeds his insatiable appetite for details of life back home in the boring provinces which he has left, and to which he is forever mentally returning, if only because she is there. The occasional sense of pique and even sadness that he expresses at her failure to maintain his (often frenzied) epistolary pace acts as a preface to so many of his letters – but he persists, uses her as a confidante, a sounding-board, a pupil, and a ready audience for whatever he has to say. Back in Grenoble, Pauline could read about the theatre wars pitting one actress against another in Paris, about the mines of Germany, or about the burning of Moscow during the 1812 campaign. Stendhal's father was too cold and distant to be the beneficiary of this constant fizzing stream of ideas, *aperçus*, observations and advice: Pauline was, instead, the ideal replacement for Stendhal's mother, who had died when he was only seven. Stendhal escaped from Grenoble to Paris, from France to Italy, Germany, England, Russia… but Pauline remains, for the most part, in Grenoble, often just as trammelled and melancholy as he would have been if cooped up there, but at least providing him with a still point of reference, the acceptable face of provincial life. She is the Good Sister, and for Stendhal the provinces are (partly) redeemed only when maternal-sororal, and not paternal. He often fantasised about living with her; he occasionally toyed with the idea of marrying (he never did), but wrote to Pauline 'I love you with all my soul, I will never love any mistress as much as you' and even envisioned living with his sister alongside a wife or mistress.

But the addressee of these letters, even though she emerges quite sharply as a character from Stendhal's letters to her (perhaps more than in her own to him) is still a figure of paper. When she was too present, when paper and ink no longer mediated between these two creatures of flesh and blood (as apparently happened on her fateful, unsuccessful trip to Italy with Stendhal in 1817: a failed attempt on his part to square the circle by bringing together two of his loves, for his sister and for Italy), she started to seem commonplace: something in the relationship between the two was broken. The last letter in this collection is a sour and frigid *envoi*: Stendhal observes to Pauline, cuttingly 'I advise you to settle down as a schoolmistress in some convent in Rome or Naples'. Her husband Daniel-François Périer-Lagrange, whom she married in May 1810 (a woman must marry, Stendhal had advised her repeatedly: but of course he soon took a considerable dislike to the man selected) proved to be bad at business and died ruined in 1816: Pauline was left in a situation of great financial constraint. (Much to Stendhal's chagrin – or rather, apoplectic rage: 'the bastard!' – their father had also died in poor financial shape, leaving his children with little by way of an inheritance.) She thereafter eked out a living. Like her brother, she did get away from Grenoble, not just for holidays but for professional reasons; she even made it as far as Paris. But there was little *stendhalien* glamour in her escape: she spent some time in Enghien-les-Bains, just north of Paris, where she worked as a spa attendant in the thermal baths. But the provinces reclaimed her, and she returned to Grenoble, where she died, practically destitute, in 1857, having outlived her brother by some fifteen years.

I have included only three of her letters here: either Stendhal's complaints about her never writing were justified, or many of her letters have been lost. Either way, those that have been published are generally similar in tone to the examples I have given: sensitive, a little melancholy, resentful of being stuck at home, occasionally sharply observant. So she complains about the 'hardness of heart' and hypocrisy of her family and the cultural backwardness of life in the Dauphiné region: amazingly, two and a half centuries after the publication of Copernicus' *De revolutionibus orbium coelestium*, both she and Stendhal were still being taught the Ptolemaic system of astronomy by their tutor, the Abbé Raillane, a man with a heart as black as his cassock – in the view of his charges, at least. She takes refuge from these cramping circumstances (being her brother's sister) in the beauties of the local landscape, and in reading 'Shakespeare or Ossian' (those were the days when this conjunction did not seem at all bizarre) by a nearby waterfall. She ends the same letter (4th September 1805) on a more stoic note, and shows that she is quite capable of deriving amusement from the pomposities of Dauphinois worthies – she has something of her brother's satirical eye for these comic personages. But her boredom was at times anguished (letter of 5th December 1805) and she plays with the idea of shooting herself. A teenage pose? Possibly: but the *ennui* of the Grenoble winter, even with moonlight and Shakespeare for company, must have been intense.

Stendhal's advice to his sister could be as contradictory as everything else about him. He both encouraged her to be independent, and advised caution (she was a young woman and could not expect to enjoy the same independent lifestyle as he did, he condescendingly, but realistically, told her); her moments of rebellion (such as her illicit excursion to Voreppe, the home of their grandfather – something to which Stendhal refers in his letter of 29th August 1804) call forth from him cries of alarm, partly real and partly feigned; and even when he mentions Mary Wollstonecraft (in the letter of 29th August 1804), who had recently published her *Vindication of the Rights of Women*, it is in a context where the emphasis is on the feminine *Realpolitik* involved in having to make at least temporary accommodations with the established patriarchal order. So he warns her (in the letter of 18th November 1807) that her penchant for dressing up in male attire might just conceivably, in stuffy old Grenoble, spoil her marriage chances… There have been speculations that, although Pauline had several affairs with men, she was lesbian, or half lesbian, or overly inclined to *amitiés amoureuses* with women – though dressing up as a man might simply have been a way of getting out and about incognito and unchaperoned. Either way, the originality of her character was never allowed to flourish as her brother's was.

Stendhal's letters refer to many of the same anecdotes, tastes, works of art, landscapes, and historical events as do his overtly autobiographical writings, such as his diaries or his *Life of Henry Brulard*. The accounts differ – and it is often difficult to know which one is the more trustworthy. The letters seem to have the stamp of improvisation, intimacy, and authenticity: why would Stendhal wish to deceive or mislead his beloved sister? Even so, the letters are as much part of the act as his endlessly digressive, endlessly self-ironising autobiographies (which will proclaim something as true on page ten only to deny it on page fifteen). But the man whose published works were signed by a hundred pseudonyms signs his letters to his sister, too, with a host of different names: the man known to the register of births of his local parish as 'Marie-Henri Beyle' writes at the foot of his letters to Pauline 'Henri', or 'H.', or 'H. Beyle', or (prefixed by a whole range of titles such as 'Sub-Lieutenant'), Lecoeur, Durand, Foulques, the Président de Brosses, Sorbon, Dufour, Dubois, D'Alrimple, Odile Watier, F. Brenier, F. Maisseano… These pseudonyms are not here marked out by any substantial difference in style of writing, or mode of being, as are the pseudonyms of, say, Kierkegaard and Pessoa: they simply add a frisson of role-playing: *don't read me too straight*. Conversely, though his letters, his diaries and autobiographical writings, his travelogues and his narrative fictions all seem to fit into different genres, it is *one* tone of voice – quizzical, alert, self-possessed and self-questioning, assertive and sceptical, passionate and disabused, that spills across all of them.

And the language of the letters to Pauline, at least in French, fizzes and crackles. They are never 'witty' (Stendhal was wary of that quality, for all his later reputation as a brilliant salon *causeur*), but they are 'fast', *allegro vivace, con brio,* never lingering, always darting from one subject to another, mixing off-the-cuff remarks (sometimes literally: Stendhal had a habit of jotting down ideas on his clothes) with book reviews, observations on logic, and snapshots of war-torn Europe. Many of the earlier letters are annotated book-lists, interspersed with accounts of life in the theatres and salons of Paris, or of his latest love affairs. These letters also give us vivid, often eyewitness accounts of some of the most momentous events in that tumultuous period, and they are scored through with traces of the history of their time: Stendhal's early letters to Pauline are addressed to 'Citoyenne' and dated according to the French Revolutionary calendar; Republic is replaced by Empire, Napoleon rises and falls (and Stendhal, as he liked to point out, rises and falls with him – though Stendhal, enraged at Napoleon's final exile by perfidious Albion, at least manages, unlike his hero, to rise again, to the not-so-heady heights of a post as French Consul in Civitavecchia, a one-horse town only slightly less claustrophobic than St Helena…). And by the time the last of these letters was written, in 1825, the autocratic and reactionary Charles X, a Bourbon, was yet again on the throne of France.

Stendhal taught Pauline history by taking part in it, as well as by urging her to read as many works about history as he himself could devour. He encouraged her to learn Italian as he did: like many good teachers, he kept just a few lessons ahead of his pupil. I have included one of Stendhal's letters in a more than passable Italian, and several in which he deploys an English idiom that might be called 'Anglo-Beylish': with its orthographical weirdness, its grammar stranded midway between Dover and Calais, and its sometimes nervy jokiness, it can convey a lapidary, conspiratorial poetry ('Speack to self-love and vanity. Make our uncle an auxiliary power' – in the letter of 7th August 1810), splutter with indignation at paternal stinginess (in the same letter, Stendhal insists that his father actually has 'sex thousand livers' – *livres* or pounds, one assumes – that he could dig into to help Stendhal out), or sigh with longing (the letter of 14th July 1812): 'I will see again my dear Italy. It is my true country'. Is there any rationale to his use of Anglo-Beylish? Sometimes it is a pedagogic device (Stendhal as language instructor), sometimes a kind of code (rather like Pepys's French) to evade prying eyes (of family or, given the demands of censorship in Stendhal's time, of state – but it was a pretty transparent code, and it is doubtful that, for instance, Chérubin Beyle would have been all that mystified to see himself identified as 'the father' rather than 'le père'). Perhaps it was all just for fun – child's play, a way of lightening up the letters when they became too didactic, or resentful, or 'dry'. It is certainly nice to have him Gallicising, for Pauline's ear, the name of England's premier poet as 'Chéquspire'.

More than anything, his way with English spelling and grammar enables him both to flirt with another language and to try out, however fleetingly, a new identity for himself. And this is all part of the act. But, for all the wearing of masks, the mystification and role-playing, the multiple pseudonyms, Henri Beyle never signs himself in these letters to Pauline with the pseudonym that has become most closely associated with him: Stendhal. Only in 1817 did a work appear in the Paris bookshops under the title *Rome, Naples et Florence, en 1817*, by one 'M. de Stendhal, Officier de Cavalerie'. An odd choice: as an Italianophile who disliked the German language (see the first letter of 1807 below), it might not have been expected that Beyle would select the name of a German town (Stendal) which he may or may not have visited – choosing it, apparently, because it had been the birthplace of the art historian Winckelmann (by whom he was inspired, but with whose views of art he profoundly disagreed). But Stendhal he became: this was the name by which he signed the works of his maturity. And it was around this time, 1817 – when he was establishing himself, however pseudonymously, as an author – that his correspondence with Pauline started to slacken. She had been a ready audience for all those years: but now he had a wider potential readership – one which he often envisaged gaining only posthumously. The great novels (*The Red and the Black*, *The Charterhouse of Parma*, *Lucien Leuwen*) all post-date the years in which Pauline was his regular confidante. There is something a little poignant in this – and in the alienation that overtook one of the most affectionate brother-sister relationships in literary history. But Pauline (perhaps precisely by having to stay at home and thus keeping alive an ideal of 'the provincial' that was not just staid, stuffy and stifling but loving, loyal, and passionate) had unwittingly helped 'my good Henri', 'my dear friend', through his long appren-ticeship. Still, it would be wrong to see Stendhal's letters to Pauline as merely the launch-pad for his sky-rocketing novels. Writing was writing for Stendhal, whether it was a jotting on his braces, the spidery annotations to a sketch map of a battlefield, or a letter to Pauline. There are novelistic bits in these letters, and letter-to-Pauline moments in the fiction. And though the 'great novels' have their own closure (style, irony, and myth), even they were only ever, for this eternal beginner, yet another apprenticeship.

– Andrew Brown, 2011

Note on the text
In the following, […] indicates cuts that I have made; [***] indicates either an ellipsis of Stendhal's, or a part of the letter that has been cut out or otherwise made illegible. Passages of Stendhal's letters in bold were written in his (rather original) English in the original: I have preserved his spellings. More generally, I have tried to mimic the spon-taneity – at times scrappy, at times eloquent – of his letters. The foot-notes, unhappily many, give some details of the people and places Stendhal refers to: the happy few will ignore them.

I have used Stendhal, *Lettres intimes* (Paris: Calmann Lévy, 1892), *Lettres à Pauline* (Paris: Le Divan, 1947) and *Oeuvres complètes* (Le Divan, 1927–37); and I have consulted with pleasure the works of two fine biographers, Victor del Litto and Jonathan Keates.

Letters to Pauline

Paris, 18th Ventose Year VIII [9th March 1800][1]

I hardly know what to say, my dear Pauline, when I reflect that I've actually gone five whole months without writing to you. I've been thinking I must do so for some time now, but I've had so many things on that I haven't got round to satisfying my desire. To begin with, I want you to write to me every week, without fail; if you don't,[2] I'll scold you; then I want you not to show your letters, or mine, to anybody; when I'm writing from the heart, I don't want to feel trammelled. You can tell me how you're getting on with the piano; whether you're taking dancing lessons. Have you been dancing this winter? I imagine so. Are you taking drawing lessons? The devil who sticks his nose into my business has stopped me having any ever since I arrived. I'm taking dancing lessons from a dancer at the Opéra; his style is completely different from Beler's; since the style I'm learning is the right one and, as such, will sooner or later reach the provinces, my advice is that you prepare for it – you have to bend at each step, and make sure you kick your heels up properly. I dance with Adèle Rebuffel;[3] she's only eleven, but she has plenty of talent and spirit. One of the things that's contributed the most to giving her both these qualities is the fact she's an avid reader; I'd like you to follow the same route, as I'm convinced it's the only worthwhile one. If you choose your reading matter wisely, you will find it so fascinating that you'll fall in love with it – and it will lead you to the true philosophy. This is an inexhaustible source of supreme pleasure; it strengthens the soul and gives us the necessary capacity to sense genius, and to love and worship it. With philosophy, all difficulties are smoothed out, all obstacles removed; the soul becomes vaster, it can understand and love more deeply. But I'm talking to you in a new, strange language; I hope you may grasp my meaning one day. I advise you to ask grandfather to get La Harpe's *Cours de littérature* from Chalvet, who must have a copy.[4] And read it; you may find it a bit boring, but it'll tidy your ideas up and I promise you that you'll reap the rewards later on. I also advise you to look out for the notes I took on literature – you'll read the same things as in La Harpe, and at the same time. This is a vital thing to study, as you'll see when you go into any society worth the name. I'd like you to go to the theatre from time to time, to see a few select plays; I'm convinced that nothing forms one's taste better. Above all, I'd like you to see some good comic operas; this would give you a taste for music and you'd derive boundless pleasure from it; but do remember that you'll only ever be able to go with Papa. If he could follow my reasoning, I'd be delighted. I'll talk it over with him when I go to Grenoble. I advise you to try and read the *Lives of the Great Men of Greece* by Plutarch; you'll find out, when you are more advanced in literature, that reading this author was what shaped the character of the man who had the most beautiful soul ever, and the greatest genius: Jean-Jacques Rousseau. You can read Racine, and Voltaire's tragedies, if you're allowed to do so. Ask my grandfather to read you *Zadig*, as he read it to me two years ago. I'd also recommend that you read *Le Siècle de Louis XIV*, if that's acceptable.[5] You'll say: what a lot of things to read! But, my dear, it's by reading thoughtful books that we learn to think and feel in our turn. In any case, read La Harpe. Farewell. I can't write any more on this paper; I preferred to try this evening rather than leave it for a few days.

Paris, 20th Germinal Year VIII [10th April 1800]

I haven't the slightest idea why you haven't replied, my dear Pauline. Whatever can be keeping you so busy that you can't write? I'd guess it must be dancing lessons, if we weren't in the middle of Lent. But I'll bet you one thing: in your view, you have to plan your letter and write out a rough draft; this is the stupidest habit anyone can get into; to have a good epistolary style, you have to write down exactly what you would say to the person if you saw them, taking care not to repeat things, even when the accent of one's voice or one's gestures could make such repetition more useful in conversation. […]

How's the piano? And the lessons with the nuns? Try to get someone to teach you some maths – it's the most essential thing of all. If I were at Grenoble, I'd be happy to take on the job myself; since I'm not there, I think M. David could give you a few lessons; it wouldn't cost Papa much and it would be extremely useful to you.

I think that, if you take four or five lessons every *décade*,[6] it would all cost 6 or 9 francs per month, and, after ten months, for a mere forty francs or so, you'd have learned to reason better than many men. Tell me what you think; and, if you like the idea, I'll suggest it to Papa, or you can ask him yourself. This would be a better thing for you than 40 years with your nuns and 50 pairs of stockings. A girl who plans to be a good mother must know how to sew a stocking and never touch a needle, especially in the precious days of her youth; your education will probably come to an end at the age of twenty; now, if you've spent two hours knitting, during that time you could have read two hundred and fifty pages of a useful book, and what a difference there is between the two! Bear in mind that six francs will pay for a pair of stockings, and nothing can make up for the thirty or forty hours of labour and the ten or twelve hours of boredom it involves. [...]

H.

Milan, 10th Messidor, Year VIII of the Republic [29th June 1800]

I was most touched, my dear Pauline, by the short letter you wrote to me; I only wish it had been a bit longer. I hope I don't have to complain about this forever. As you know, I'm in Milan, it's a city as big as five Grenobles, quite attractively built. There's a church in gothic style, i.e. all in filigree patterns arranged in vaults rather than in fully rounded arches – it's impressive when you think about it, but it doesn't grab you right from the start like the sublime Panthéon.[7] I think the summit of the building is higher than the gallery of the Panthéon. To get an idea, you need to imagine a circular gallery fifty to sixty feet long and as high as four of Saint-André's spires placed on top of each other.[8] The church isn't finished yet and probably never will be; inside, it isn't particularly beautiful on the whole, just an astonishing monument to the infinite patience it required from the various different workers who contributed to building it; there are maybe a thousand statues, from forty feet in size down to six inches. I won't tell you about the Mont Saint-Bernard, you can read a description of it one day in any of the thousand and one trips to Italy. All I can tell you is that its difficulty has been greatly exaggerated. There isn't a moment's danger for the men crossing it. I passed in front of the fort at Bard, a much more difficult mountain.[9] Imagine a steeply sided setting like that of the valley of Saint-Paul, near Claix.[10] In the middle, a low hillock; on that hillock, a fort; the road leads to the fort straight along the bottom of the valley, passing under the fort within pistol shot. We left it about six hundred yards from the fort and climbed the mountain under continual fire from the fort. What gave us the greatest difficulty was our horses; every time a bullet or a shell came whistling past, they dashed five or six feet forward. I don't know if you can follow this description, but I want you to share this truly amazing spectacle, and I have only a moment to write it down for you. There's a superb theatre here. Imagine an interior as big as half of the Place Grenette.[11] They perform the same opera for a fortnight; the music is divine and the actors awful. All the box seats are rented out, so all that leaves for us is the stalls and the box that's set aside for army staff. I'm putting a great deal of effort into learning Italian, but as I haven't found a [***], progress is slow. In any case, I'm being kept busy and can't work on it as much as I'd like. I've formed a much better impression of the Italians than the one that's widespread in France; I've made friends with one or two who, quite honestly, astonish me with the wisdom of their ideas and the sense of honour that reigns in their hearts. One thing I was far from expecting is the charm and kindness of the women of this country. You'll never believe me, but really, right now, I'd just hate to have to return to Paris. We are suffering terribly from the very oppressive heat. At first we'd thought we could keep it at bay by stuffing ourselves with ice creams, but we discovered that they actually made us feel even hotter after cooling us down for a moment. I hope you'll reply to this long letter. Address your reply to Milan. I hope to be still here, or in the environs, when your letter arrives.

H. Beyle

[...] We are suffering from the terrible heat, it is too much for a Frenchman, we all find it oppressive. I recently took a rather pleasant trip that meant I could get away for a few days from the scorching open squares here. I went with Daru[12] to receive the fortress at Arona,[13] and I took this opportunity to visit the divine Borromean Islands; there are three of them – *Isola Bella*, *Isola Madre*, *Isola dei Pescatori*. Imagine a semi-circular lake, some fifteen leagues long; the part facing Milan, or rather Buffalora, is surrounded by charming slopes. The Tessino, a superb river, flows out from this part of the lake; as you advance across these tranquil waves, the slopes turn into mountains, and the part of the lake next to Switzerland is surrounded by beetling rocks that resemble the Mont St Bernard. The lakeside here is tranquil; few houses, no agriculture, no trace of those horrid trellises, those palisades that disfigure the famous shores of Lake Geneva. Here you can see nature on all sides; from time to time you encounter a small bark with two fishermen in it. On you go for an hour and a half; all of a sudden you turn round and find that you're at the foot of the fortress and the town of Arona. I've never seen a more impressive vista. Imagine an escarpment like the one at the Porte de France[14] in Grenoble, on the one side; and on the other, a gentle slope; at the summit, an impregnable fort surrounded by five successive walls that make it impossible to assail, a slender, lofty tower, and, floating on top, the *tricolore*. All of a sudden, nineteen cannon shots are fired, and clods of earth come raining down into the lake and sully for a moment its limpid waters. We go down, after struggling for three quarters of an hour against quite a violent hail of shots. The following morning, after visiting the fort, we re-embark on some Austrian gunboats; we leave a small port surrounded by waves; we head out into the lake, and straightaway a superb statue of good Saint Charles[15] draws our attention; it's sixty-nine feet high, and is majestically pointing with one hand to the port; with the other, Saint Charles holds a fold of his surplice; you go in through this fold. A man can stand upright in the statue's nose; the statue is quite tranquil in the middle of the lake. It had been quite undisturbed for a good long while when, just recently, at the siege of Arona, a cannon ball hit it in the chest, but luckily it wasn't damaged. Never have I seen such a lovely vista: words cannot express what I felt. We were sailing gently along, I was next to the admiral of the enemy fleet, and chatting with one of Melas's[16] aides-de-camp, a charming young man, give or take a few prejudices. After three hours' sail, we saw, in the middle of this divine lake, a green mountain, and on the right a beach and a small white house. The island on the left is *Isola Bella*. The one on the right is *Isola Madre*. But I can see that I'm rambling; never mind. Since you are starting to get an idea of this romantic situation, you can weave your way through its enchanting sights in your mind. But above all, don't show this letter to anybody, now that I think of it, as it will strike the cold-hearted as perfectly ridiculous. A big hug.

B.

Bagnolo, 16th Frimaire Year IX [7th December 1800]

[...] I'm with my regiment in a wretched little cisalpine village, three leagues away from Brescia. We have absolutely none of the things we need, and the worst of it is that the colonel can't give us permission to go to Brescia, since we're expecting to launch an attack from one minute to the next. Sometimes we don't have any bread, and then we're reduced to eating *polenta*, the usual food of those brutes with human faces that dwell in this region. I've never seen, and had never imagined, men as brutish as the Italian lower classes. They are every bit as ignorant as our peasants, and in addition they have false and treacherous hearts, and are filthy cowards and the most obnoxious fanatics. I'm not surprised that impiety was born in Italy: even the best religion would arouse hatred if it had proselytes such as these. Recently, the Grand Vicar, who is responsible for the armies in this canton, issued them with a little sermon unique in its genre. If I'd managed to lay my hands on a copy, I'd have sent it to you; although it's in Italian, grandfather could have translated it for you; it stated, after uttering every possible lamentation against the impious French, that the cows whose milk we drank would all die, that if anyone gave us wine, the vines from which the wine had come would all wither, and finally that the houses we lodged in would be consumed by lightning. It would be possible

8

to console oneself for these absurdities if this was all there was, but as soon as a Frenchman wanders off into the fields, there's a hail of bullets; the hussars of the 10th found the priest of the next village, where they are stationed, setting fire to the farms to drive us away. As you can see, we are surrounded by men of goodwill... I can assure you that we miss France and Switzerland; at least if we were there, we'd have real men to deal with. We don't even have any books. All we do to pass the time is go hunting, when the everlasting rain allows it. Farewell. Write more often. Remember that one of your letters fills my whole day with charm. A kiss on both your cheeks.

H.B.

Milan Headquarters, 2nd Nivose Year IX [23rd December 1800]

Ho ricevuto, cara sorella, la tua lettera, che m'a fato un piacere particolare. [...] Tu sai che siamo ancora una volta le mani legate in questo maladetto paese. Il mio piu grande desiderio e de lo fugire si lontano che senta mai il suo nome vituperato. [...] Di mi se questo iverno tu vai qualche volte al spectacolo, lo desirerei molto credendo que l'odizione delle bonne comedie et tragedie forma il caratere ed impara a essere bono e bravo nel mondo perche non ce tutto di formar belli designi nella solitudine, il tutto e de l'esecutare fra tutti i pericoli che possono [***].

Ecco una superba morale, ho gran paura che t'infantidischa, ti diro cose meno inniose quando avro il piacere di comprimerti nei miei bracci.

Adio, scrive mi piu sovanti.

H.B.

[Translation:]

I have received, dear sister, your letter, which gave me a special pleasure. [...] As you know, our hands are again tied in this damned country. My greatest desire is to flee so far from it that never again will I hear its hated name. [...] Tell me if, this winter, you are sometimes going to the theatre, I'd very much hope so, as I think that hearing good comedies and

tragedies forms one's character and teaches us to be kind and good in
society, since it's not enough to lay fine plans in solitude, the main thing
is to carry them out among all the dangers that may [***].

That's a grand moral, though I'm dreadfully afraid you might find
it tedious, I'll tell you some less boring things when I have the pleasure
of hugging you in my arms.

Farewell, write to me more often.

H.B.

Milan, 6th Nivose Year IX [27th December 1800]

[...] I've come back from my regiment for a few days, but my tour
of duty has kept me in Milan for longer than I'd expected. But I hope
to get away one of these days. All the French in Milan lost their sense
of hearing three days ago; the two or three thousand bells here are
in the strangest convulsions. You can't imagine the kind of racket they
kick up. In spite of a heavy cold, which the thick fogs of Lombardy
have landed me with, I went to the theatre yesterday, it was the first
performance in the carnival season. You can't imagine the beauty of the
decorations and the splendour of the costumes; the illusion is complete
in a theatre like Milan. Imagine the Place Grenette covered over and all
the balconies with taffeta drapes of every colour; the smallest theatre
boxes are as big as the small room I used to sleep in when I was in
Grenoble. In their boxes, everyone has lighted candles, a table, cards,
and usually you can order refreshments to be brought in for the ladies.
Do you sometimes go dancing during the carnival? Are you learning
history? That's what I want you to study, since then you'll be able to
read travellers' accounts and, thanks to them, study the manners and
customs of our neighbours.

I hope that this time you will break your silence. When you write
to me, give your letters to Marion, who will easily find an opportunity
to post them.[17] If you could only imagine the pleasure I derive from
four lines of your handwriting, you wouldn't give me this charming
pleasure as rarely as you do.

Tell me what Caroline[18] is up to. My grandfather has told me he was
going to teach her Latin, to spur Gaëtan into emulating her.[19] I hope

this plan works out, but I doubt it. I'm afraid our sister is a narrow-minded hypocrite, and our cousin is a clumsy oaf. As for you, my dear, my only sister, try to rise above the miasmas that darken your path as you disembogue into society. Be kind and loving and, above all, never pretend; it's a crime to feign virtue. Farewell. A heartfelt hug from me. Write to me, please!

H.B.
Sub-Lieutenant

To check whether this letter has been opened, look and see if the seal clearly shows the head of a young man, his head wreathed with a crown of olives – Francis II, the current monarch.[20]

Cocalio,[21] *3rd Ventose Year IX [22nd February 1801]*

I left Milan yesterday, my dear Pauline and after a march of two days I have finally reached the foot of my beloved mountains. I'm in a small town three leagues from Brescia, with the great range of the Alps rising behind it, placed in a kind of amphitheatre on a pretty mountain slope which, as far as I can tell at seven o'clock in the evening, is covered with vines. The road from Milan here must be divine in summer, as it is pretty enough in winter; you have the mountains on the left, and imposing factory buildings every so often occupy the vista to the right. When I'd had enough of gazing at the countryside, I remembered the soil I was treading. Seven thousand Russians perished in the retreat of [***] while trying to storm the bridge at Cassano that I crossed this morning.[22] You can still see, in a chapel to the right of the bridge, several hundred heads. This is where I learned one of the reasons for the bravery of this credulous and superstitious people. Suvorov had managed to get their chaplains to persuade them that all of those who died of a wound to the front of their bodies went to heaven, whereas those who perished from a wound in the back went down to hell. From here I can make out a small fortress built at Rocafrana on Bonaparte's orders. They say that you can get a lovely view from this place. I really regret that I can't devote a couple of hours to doing so. I learnt en route, from two officers, that my general had transferred his headquarters to Mantua. So that's the town to which I am heading and I hope to get your reply there, since I hope you eventually will reply. I bet you're going to regret not living in Milan when you learn that, by special favour of the Pope, as made public in an *ad hoc* papal bull, the carnival has been prolonged by four days in that fortunate town; and as young girls are the same everywhere, they make a point of flocking there from Ash Wednesday onwards. This makes the four last masked balls charming occasions, and I can assure you that the one I attended three days ago is almost the equal of those I saw in Paris a year ago. [...]

H.B.

I've nearly reached my destination, my dear Pauline, since there are just two and a half leagues of marshland between myself and Mantua. I'm eager to see this town, so famous for the two sieges it sustained in year IV and year VII. It's surrounded by water in this rainy season. You reach it via a plain that greatly resembles that around the Rondeau;[23] here and there you see several fields that resemble the marshes of Claix. Castiglione, where I dined, is situated at the very foot of the mountains, and the main streets in town are rather like the steep road up to Chalemont.[24] There's a fort there. I won't say anything about Brescia, it's a collection of more or less attractive houses, like any other town, and nothing looks more frigid than those heaps of stone. What I enjoy seeing in a town are its inhabitants, since an observer can always find something interesting about his fellow men, and there are certain countries where even the coldest man will be struck dumb with amazement. In Brescia there are three hundred and twenty-one houses for monks and nuns, apart from the parish church and a bishopric. A man can be killed stone dead for a couple of ducats – about eight French francs; if he's still alive after the dagger blow, the real assassin will give as much as four ducats (sixteen francs) to his henchman. You will observe that Brescia is a town of twenty-eight or thirty thousand souls, and every month there are between sixty and eighty murders; under the *ancien régime*, the number rose to ninety or a hundred.

Paris is a city of eight to nine hundred thousand souls where, in consequence, excesses of every kind are most common, which ought to give rise to many murders. When I was there, a year ago, there were fifty-seven churches of every kind, tolerated by the government, and, according to the reports of the Minister of Police, on working days some three to four hundred worshippers attended each church and, on Sundays, from one thousand five hundred to two thousand; there were usually ten or fifteen murders, seven to eight suicides and fifteen to twenty deaths in duels; so every day, society lost some forty persons who died by violence, which makes one thousand two hundred per month. This number of violent deaths in Paris, that sink of all corruption, is thus half what it is in a little town in Italy. I'm not including in the Brescia figures either the suicides nor those killed in a duel; Italians rarely perish in this manner.

Farewell, write to me at Mantua, HQ of the reserve.

H.B.

Bergamo, 19th Floréal Year IX [9th May 1801]

You have sometimes been to Montfleury, my dear Pauline; from there you have admired the enchanting spectacle presented by that valley watered by the winding river Isère.[25] If you have ever been there during a thunderstorm, when the black clouds are locked in combat and tear each other apart, when heaven and earth echo to the rumble of the thunder, when the rain mingled with hail sweeps all before it, your soul has doubtless risen towards the father of the clouds and the earth. You have sensed the power of the Creator; but, little by little, this sublime idea has given way to a sweet melancholy, you have come back to your own self and thought of your plans for happiness, you have become absorbed in them, and you have been sorry at the end of the storm and the need to return home. Well, imagine a plain forty leagues across, watered by the Tessino, the Adda, the Mincio and the majestic Po; imagine a dark night in mid-summer, two hundred claps of thunder in half an hour, real fiery clouds darting from a dark sky and flashing across the atmosphere in two seconds, and you will have just a feeble idea of the magnificent tempest I saw this morning.

Never have I laid eyes on a more wonderful spectacle, and the twelve or fifteen comrades I had with me confessed that they had never seen anything so impressive. We saw a bolt of lightning falling on a church tower at our feet – the whole town of Bergamo is like the slope up to Chalemont. We're on ground level when we go in from behind, and on the tenth floor at least when we get to the front. As you see, we're at the foot of the Alps and we can see the Apennines. [...]

H.B.

So, my dear Pauline, it's decided that you're not going to write to me any more? It's been five months since I received any news from you directly. So give me some news, tell me in detail what you're up to, as well as Caroline. Grandfather has told me that you were both at Mlle Lassaigne's[26] where, from what he told me, you were brought up on the basis of excellent principles. So give me lots of details. Tell me, please, about all the books you're reading, tell me if you enjoy them and what you think of them. Are you studying history – not the history that consists of learning M. Le Ragois[27] by heart, but that philosophical history that shows, in all events, the sequence of men's passions and demonstrates, from the experience of every age, that if one is to be happy, one must intend the good, and do it? What's become of Félicie?[28] Is she as intelligent as she was promising to be two years ago? How has Caroline turned out? Has she rid herself of that detestable tone of bigotry that she had picked up in that terrible school?

You can see from the frankness of the questions I'm asking you that you need to keep my letter to yourself. Please reply at length to all my inquiries. For two years we have been strangers to each other; you were very young then, but now that you have become reasonable, I'd really like you to regard me as one of your best friends, and to write to me more often.

A while ago I asked Papa to be so good as to send me the shirts that Aunty kindly ran up for me, as well as a few pairs of stockings. Please ensure these things are sent to me soon. It's devilish cold in this country, and a poor convalescent really needs to wrap up warm. Farewell.

H. B.

Paris, Messidor Year X [July 1802]

I cannot find the words, dear Pauline, to express the pleasure your letter gave me: anyway, I can see you that are finding plenty to occupy yourself with. You have no idea how much I regret that circumstances force me to live in Paris, how much pleasure it would give me to work with you, and cultivate that soul of yours, so richly endowed. […] I am delighted to learn you are starting Italian: it will give us something else in common; I will send you, via Colomb,[29] an excellent grammar, as the one you are probably following, by M. Gatel, is just a jumble of rules.

I'm also going to send you a short book, two hundred and thirteen pages long, in-18[0], that will give you more ideas than all the libraries in the world! It's the *Logique* of our compatriot the Abbé de Condillac.[30] There's no point in talking about this outside the family; everyone would think I was crazy to send you a book like this, and they would find it presumptuous of you to even try to read it; but, my dear Pauline, let's leave the fools to blather on, and carry on regardless; even better, let's stop them carping at our behaviour by concealing our actions from them.

This logic, which people make such a fuss about, would be the easiest thing in the world if they only brought to it a mind free of prejudice: I will try to get you to understand one page per week; I am convinced that, once we've worked through the first two chapters, you'll be able to carry on by yourself.

Furthermore, my dearest, once you've read this short book of two hundred and thirteen pages, nothing will be able to hold you back in any branch of knowledge: the most difficult calculations in algebra, the most knotty points of grammar, will no longer present the slightest difficulty to you; you yourself will be amazed at the rapid progress you make in all your studies, the more you learn to reason; for logic is nothing other than the art of reasoning. […]

I'm replying straightaway, my dear Pauline, since otherwise it might be a long time before I get round to it; I have on my table eleven or twelve letters to reply to, and they've all been waiting their turn for a month; get into the habit of doing things in order early on – I'm organised only in my studies, and I very often have occasion to regret this in my social relations; make it your principle to always reply to a letter in the forty-eight hours following its arrival.

So get yourself an Italian teacher, any teacher, straightaway; and while you wait, copy out and learn off by heart the two auxiliaries *essere* and *avere*,[31] try to understand the big table at the start of your Italian grammar. My advice is that you take a big sheet of paper and copy it all out. Then you should read, every evening before you go to bed, the verb *avere*, then the verb *essere*. It's the only way to learn, I'm counting on it.

You could be reading something much better than *L'Homme des champs*.[32] It's no good. Read Racine and Corneille, Corneille and Racine, all the time. Since you don't know Latin, you can read the *Georgics* in Delille's version. Since you can't read Homer and Virgil, you can read the *Henriade*.[33] That will give you some slight idea of the kind of thing those great men could write. Read La Harpe; his taste isn't reliable, but he'll give you some initial ideas, and if I ever have the good luck to spend two months with you in Claix, far from all the bores, we'll talk literature. I'll tell you how I view things and I hope you'll feel the same way about them. You have the ability to become a charming woman, but you need to get used to thinking things through – that's the great secret.

To get a proper sense of the rhythm of poetry, you have to attune your ear to it. I'd like you to look up the fourth act of *Iphigénie*, scene four, and to learn the tirade that starts with these words: 'My father', to 'that I shall relate to them'.[34] I advise you to copy them out and read them in the evening. It's quite essential to read poetry out properly, and I'd like you to know all of Iphigénie's role by next September; I'll teach you to declaim it. In the case of Corneille, you can restrict yourself to reading the following plays: *Le Cid*, *Horace*, *Cinna*, *Rodogune* and

Polyeucte. Ask Grandpapa to lend you *Le Misanthrope* by Molière. You can read *Rhadamiste et Zénobie*, by Crébillon, *Mérope*, *Zaïre* and *La Mort de César*, by Voltaire.[35] If you have good taste, you will place Corneille and Racine in the front rank of French tragedians, Voltaire and Crébillon in the second. Finally let me recommend you to keep reading Racine and Corneille ceaselessly, I am like the Church, there is no salvation outside them.

Enjoyment of them brings its own reward.[36]

H.B.

Paris, 11th Nivose Year XI [1st January 1803]

> *Weary of being a slave, of drinking deep*
> *The dregs of life (it is a bitter cup);*
> *Since poverty is viewed with foolish scorn,*
> *I often yearn for death, the restful tomb*
> *And far-off country from whose friendly bourn*
> *No traveller need return [...]*[37]

Don't you feel this poetry gently penetrating into your soul, suffusing it and overmastering it? In my view, these lines seem the most touching that I have ever read in any language. I wanted to copy them straightaway while they were still present to my mind, and to send them in my first letter; but I'm sitting at my table, I have half an hour to myself, how can I fail to write to the woman I wish I could always speak to? I am planning to go and see you at the beginning of Thermidor; at first I wanted to go a month later, but what a crazy idea! We have so few days to live, and perhaps many fewer to spend together! Let us make haste to enjoy life, let us live together, let us while away our days in the bosom of friendship. True, I'm learning things here; but how cold is all knowledge in comparison with feeling! Seeing that man was not strong enough to be forever feeling, God decided to give him knowledge so as to give him some respite from passions during his youth, and to keep him busy during his last days.

Unhappy and greatly to be pitied is the cold heart that knows only how to know! Ah, what use is it to me to know that the sun revolves around the earth, or the earth around the sun, if, in learning these things, I waste the days that have been granted me to enjoy such things? Such is the folly of so many men, my dear Pauline; but it will not be ours.

I was forgetting to tell you who wrote these sweet lines I'm sending you: André Chénier composed this poem shortly before the Terror in which he perished.

I don't want to stay a single day in Grenoble, since nothing makes the soul suffer so much as to feel its [***] shrivelling. I'm living on the sixth floor, but opposite that [***] colonnade of the Louvre. Every evening, I see in succession the sun, the moon and all the stars setting behind those galleries that witnessed the events of the great seventeenth century. I imagine I can see the shades of the Great Condé,[38] Louis XIV, Corneille and Pascal hidden behind those great columns, watching with a certain interest as men, their descendants, go by, and promising to the unhappy a place of refuge among them.

As soon as I arrive, we'll go to Claix, where we'll expound Tasso, if you know Italian. […]

Paris, 2nd Pluviose Year XI [22nd January 1803]

My dear Pauline, yesterday I wrote to Papa to ask him to send me various items of clothing. Please, as a matter of urgency, do everything you possibly can to get them sent to me as soon as possible. Just think…

Without a shudder can this grim tale be heard?[39]

… that since I don't have a costume, I have had to turn down eleven delightful balls in twenty days. Now you know that, I don't have to say another word; I can already see you dashing off to send me my cravats and my silk stockings. Ask my Papa to send me another dozen pairs of gloves, six white, six yellow. Since I come from Grenoble, everyone is asking me for them, and these silly little trifles often bear fruit.

One of these days I'll write you an eight-page letter, four pages on English and your studies in general. I have only one thing to say to you: there are only two means of escaping boredom when you are not leading an active life: either find a man of wit whose conversation amuses you, or a book you can enjoy. But there are a thousand reasons why the man whose company you might enjoy is never there, and in any case, such men are hard to find; if you like reading, you'll find sources of pleasure everywhere. I've often reflected that, if men should enjoy reading, women should adore it. Look at how stupid the fifty-year-old women are in Grenoble, and how bored. Well, here, I go every Tuesday to spend the evening at the home of a woman of sixty-two. There are several pleasant people there, and yet I am never so happy as when I am sitting on the step of her carriage making her laugh with my observations on human wisdom. There are ten of us men who attend her salon and feel the same way. What fate would you prefer: that of the boring, gossipy, prudish old woman of Grenoble, or that of the delightful woman of Paris? […]

I strongly recommend that, each evening, you read an act from a play by Racine; this is the only way to speak French, and don't go thinking that people speak it properly in Grenoble; I am finding it extremely difficult to correct my way of speaking; in Grenoble, people say: *il fallait que j'allas* instead of *il fallait que j'allasse*.[40]

In Grenoble they say *pére*, *mére*, *bétise*; but it's pronounced *père*, *mère*, *bêtise*, as if it were written *paire*, *maire*, *baitise*;[41] in general, you yourself don't pronounce the accents, and since they're actually there you ought to bring them out.

Farewell, once I start writing to you, I can't stop. Please don't forget to send off my things, and to read Racine.

Paris, 9th Pluviose Year XI [29th January 1803]

I'm feeling rather low, my dear Pauline: I've come along to console myself with you. I'm going to tell you about the moral principles of literature, in other words, about what constitutes the beautiful, and what has led great men to produce the beautiful. As I don't write a rough draft of my letters first, it's possible that, for all the care I take to be clear, you won't understand me to begin with; so I suggest you keep my letters; but make sure you don't let anyone else see them. You can read them to Caroline.

Apart from geometry, there is only one way of reasoning: on the basis of the facts.

If you look through the list of great men in every domain, you soon see that poor nations have always been both more avid for glory and more fertile in great men than opulent nations. The happiest peoples are the poor peoples, for they are the most virtuous, and there is only one path to happiness on this earth: virtue. The wicked sometimes appear to be happy when viewed from a distance; but when you look more closely at them, you see that they are consumed by fear and remorse. On this point, remember Pygmalion, that cruel King of Tyre, depicted in *Télémaque*.[42] The more needs a man has, the more he exposes himself to tyranny; the more needs a woman has, the more she exposes herself to vice.

In England, there is an *opposition* party often formed by people of virtue; ask for details from Grandpapa and Papa. This opposition party is opposed to the party at Court, which is forever striving to increase the power of the king, and consequently to turn England first into a monarchy and then a despotic state. About forty years ago, Mr Walpole, the king's minister, tried to bring a certain honest gentleman in the opposition over into the Court party. So he goes to see him.

'I have come,' Mr Walpole tells him, 'from the King, to assure you of his protection, to express his regret at not having done anything for you, and to offer you a post befitting your merit.'

'My Lord,' the citizen replied to him, 'before I reply to your offer, allow me to have my supper brought before you.'

Whereupon he was served with a stew made with the leftovers from the leg of lamb he had dined from. Then, turning to Mr Walpole, he added:

'My Lord, do you think that a man who is content with a meal like this is the kind of man that the Court can easily win over? Tell the King what you have seen; this is the only answer I have for him.'

Mr Walpole withdrew in consternation. If that man had liked big meals, you can safely bet that he'd have been tempted.

There are two things that have made me study. One is the fear of boredom and the other is the love of glory. It was the desire to amuse myself or the fear of boredom that made me love reading from the age of twelve. The house was distinctly gloomy; I started to read and I was immediately happy: passions are the only things that motivate men; they produce all the good, and they are all the evil, that we see on earth.

You feel passion for an object when you desire it continually; you have a strong passion for this same object when life seems unbearable without it. This explains the behaviour of Curtius who, in Rome, flung himself into the chasm that had opened up in the middle of the main square: he preferred the people's happiness, and glory, to life, and he killed himself.[43]

Pierre Corneille would rather not have lived at all than live without glory, and he wrote *Cinna*.

Demosthenes could not live without being a great orator, but he had a stammer: anyone else would have given up when faced with this obstacle; but he placed little pebbles in his mouth and off he went to spend a couple of hours by the sea every day.[44]

Great passions can overcome all obstacles: thus one can say that when a man wants something *intensely* and *constantly*, he will reach his aim.

To try to understand something, you have to fix your whole attention on it. […]

Good evening!

Paris, 10th Pluviose Year XI [30th January 1803]

I am writing to you again, my dear Pauline, and again it's to cure myself of my mounting impatience. Here, at theatre doors, on the days when there's something interesting on, what is called a *queue* forms – a long line, in other words, of theatregoers who buy their tickets in turn. Since the weather's very cold, it's not pleasant to have to hang around in the open waiting for two hours to get hold of a ticket for the pit. One of my friends has a servant and sent him along this evening; but he's still not back, and as I result I've spent two hours waiting. I wanted to go and see *L'Homme du jour*, a five-act play in verse, by Boissy, and *Les Femmes*, a play by Demoustier;[45] I was prepared to go to some lengths since Fleury[46] and Mlle Contat[47] are performing in both plays and I wanted some good entertainment.

As you know, I've always been afraid I'd die of consumption; any other kind of death is quite without its terrors for me; but that kind I find quite chilling. Yesterday evening, returning home at eleven o'clock, my eyes were tired and I started to practise my declamations; I burst a small vein. This morning and this evening, I've been spitting a little blood; that was all I needed to imagine I'd got consumption.

You know how my imagination trots along; but anyway, I've just been trying to be sensible about it and, instead of cursing, I've settled down to write to you: I'm going to talk about literary metaphysics again.

I've already told you that men studied only to escape from boredom. Often, when we are bored, our genius is swayed by the first object that presents itself to us. I'm going to prove as much by presenting you with some facts – the best of verifications. I'll begin by telling you about our compatriot the celebrated Vaucanson:[48] you can see a fine bust of him in the library. His mother was devout and had a spiritual director; the latter lived in a cell to which a room with the big clock served as an antechamber; the mother went to visit this spiritual director frequently; her son would accompany her as far as the antechamber; it was here that, lonely and listless, he would weep with boredom, while his mother was confessing her sins. However, since we always stay weepy and bored for as little as possible, and as, in a state of listlessness, there are no indifferent sensations, young Vaucanson was soon struck by the very regular swinging of the pendulum and decided to find out the cause: so he went over to the case of the clock; through the gaps he could see the way the cogs were meshed together, he observed part of the mechanism, guessed at the rest, planned out a similar machine, constructed it with a knife and some wood, and finally made a working clock. Buoyed by this success, he increasingly concentrated his attention on mechanics, and eventually made the famous flute-player. Ask grandfather to tell you about this great man – he knew him.

Shakespeare (in French pronounced *Chéquspire*) was a wool merchant in Stratford, England; he loved hunting, which was at the time prohibited, just as it was in France before the Revolution; he killed a doe in the park of the lord of Stratford, who fined him. He was piqued at this and stole a few doe from the lord before taking off for London. Here, penniless, he held horses at the theatre entrance, then became an actor, and eventually an author. So it was his love of hunting and the stupidity of the lord of Stratford to which he owed his genius.

It was a rather similar chance event that decided Molière to go into theatre. His grandfather enjoyed seeing plays; he often took Molière with him; the young man was leading a dissolute life: when his father saw this, he angrily asked whether they were trying to turn his son into an actor. 'If only, by God, he could be as good an actor as Monrose!' replied the grandfather.[49] Molière was struck by these words; he felt repelled by the trade of tapestry maker, and France owes its greatest comic playwright to this chance reply.

Milton, the author of the sublime *Paradise Lost*, was employed by Cromwell; this usurper died; his son Richard succeeded him; he was a clodhopper, and they drove him out of England; Milton lost his job; he was imprisoned, then released, then forced to go into exile; he withdrew to the countryside where, having nothing to do, he composed *Paradise Lost* to stave off boredom.

You acquire wit not by learning a lot of things *by heart*, but *by frequently comparing* the things you see; you need to contemplate things at length and, whatever you see, to try to find out its cause.

The Athenians exiled Aristides; did he deserve this?[50] Or, if they were jealous of him, why were they jealous?

In society, whoever knows the greatest number of tales from history, witty sayings, and curious anecdotes, is the most pleasant company. Buffon,[51] Corneille, La Fontaine did not lower themselves to this kind of thing; as a result, people were very surprised to see them failing to shine in society; only dullards were amazed at this, since they failed to take into account the fact that the wit by which you gain the admiration of posterity is very different from the wit which makes you amusing in a social circle.

I can give you these general truths:

1st: All our ideas come to us through our senses;

2nd: The greater or lesser subtlety of our five senses produces neither greater nor lesser wit. Homer, Milton were blind; Montesquieu, Buffon had very poor sight;

3rd: Education alone makes men great; consequently, if you wish to become a great genius, you can be one. You need to apply yourself to a branch of knowledge and meditate on it ceaselessly. I advise you to read and meditate on Plutarch: he will teach you history and, at the same time, enable you to know what men are like.

To acquire a great wit, you need to compare things frequently, in other words to observe, alternately and attentively, the different impression that various things of whatever kind make on you.

La Fontaine became a good fabulist by comparing a great number of the fables of the authors before him.

Compare the fable 'Master Crow' with that of 'The Animals Sick of the Plague', and tell me in one of your letters which one you prefer.

Paris, Pluviose Year XI [8th February 1803]

I've received your letter of 14th, my dear Pauline; my delight is indescribable, and I can see that we are made for each other: we have the same spirit. You're right: *Athalie* isn't Racine's best play; it's extremely immoral in the way it authorises the priest to rise up against authority and to massacre the magistrates,[52] and it's precisely through this major failing that it appeals so much to the Tartuffes of the age.

The *Grandeur des Romains* that I recommended to you is indeed the one by Montesquieu;[53] you can't read and re-read this excellent work often enough; I'll just point out to you, while we are on the subject, that the study of history is good for only two things:

The first is to give us knowledge of what men are like: this knowledge is called philosophy, a word taken from the Greek and meaning *love of wisdom*; the second is the knowledge of certain facts that are often mentioned in society – things it would be ridiculous not to know.

I hope that this second kind of use will not interest you much. I find nothing so commonplace as vanity – it's almost always the index of a petty character. The man who seeks his own esteem and that of the great men of his age should always imagine himself to be in the presence of men such as Aristides, Scipio, Caesar, etc., and once he feels he has merited their approval, he will close his ears to the yapping of ordinary churls. I would again recommend that you read Plutarch in Dacier's translation. You will see, in the Life of Brutus, Caesar's killer, what kind of a woman his wife Portia was;[54] it seems to me that she's a good deal better than the flighty feather-headed women of our day.

You gradually acquire the habits and ways of seeing of the people with whom you habitually live.

This maxim is general and brooks no exception; so make sure you do not live in the society of the animals you mentioned. Reflect on this and follow our Papa's advice.

I much prefer you to learn Italian than English; this former language is much closer to the Greek and Latin languages, the most beautiful that have ever existed: we'll speak about this at length; I'll show you that there are really only two different languages, Greek and French: the first allows inversions, the second requires the direct order. Let's suppose you wish to transmit to me this thought: 'Bacon is a great philosopher'; in French, you have to put it like this: 'Bacon is a great philosopher'; and in Greek, you could say: 'Bacon is a great philosopher'; 'Philosopher a great Bacon is'; 'Is a great philosopher Bacon'; 'Bacon philosopher a great is', etc.

You can sense how much these languages lend themselves to poetry: Italian has this advantage to a certain degree. I'll be writing soon to give you, re the study of languages, the principles of Dumarsais,[55] one of the greatest grammarians who have existed, whose eulogy you can read at the beginning of the seventh volume of the *Encyclopédie*.

The greatest of comic poets, the divine Molière, said:

A learned fool is more foolish than an ignorant fool.[56]

And indeed there is nothing worse than pretend knowledge: try to keep yourself clear of it between now and the holidays. What I recommend to you is (except for religion) to believe nothing without examining it: nothing makes a person more ridiculous than repeating the stupid things said by other people. Let's never speak about things we don't know; but when we do speak, let's say only what we believe and are ready to demonstrate. Every evening, when I get home, I spend half an hour copying out for you various passages from the best authors: I'll send it to you before long.

Our Papa has a *Dictionnaire historique des grands hommes*, which will be of the greatest help to your education; look up the lives of Homer, Virgil, Horace, Lucan, Tibullus, Tacitus, Cicero, Tasso, Ariosto, Dante, Petrarch, Machiavelli, Milton, Cervantes, Camoëns, Molière, Pierre Corneille, Racine, Shakespeare, La Fontaine, Boileau,

Montaigne, J.-J. Rousseau, Fénelon, Bossuet, Buffon, Montesquieu; twenty-seven in all, and draw up an extract of twenty lines on each of them, like this:

'J.-B. Poquelin, who later took the name *Molière*, was born in Paris in 1620 (a hundred and eighty years before 1800); he was the son of a tapestry maker employed by the King: he put on *L'Étourdi*, his first play, in 1658, when he was thirty-eight years old; he died vomiting up blood at the age of fifty-three, in 1673, and composed thirty-three plays in less than fifteen years. The best are *Tartuffe* and *Le Misanthrope*. He was the best of men, and posterity regards him as one of the greatest who ever existed.'

Once you have composed these twenty-seven lives, like that of Molière – keep them just as simple – you can copy them out into a little note-book, and re-read them from time to time; this will be of the greatest use for the course on literature that I hope to be doing with you this autumn.

After the excellent *Révolutions romaines* by Vertot,[57] I advise you to read Condillac's *Histoire*: you'll find it frigid and less amusing, but he reasons perfectly well and that is a great merit. You can read Voltaire's *Le Siècle de Louis XIV*; read La Bruyère's *Caractères*.

Fall to your knees and beg my Papa to drop the study of the astronomer Ptolemy as fast as you can; that fool the Abbé Raillane[58] was so stupid as to teach it to me, and that's the reason why my ideas about astronomy are all mixed up. Drop Ptolemy tomorrow; there's nothing more pernicious than poisoning your mind with falsehoods. Your studying Ptolemy gives me a very low opinion of the people who are making you do it; they should get themselves a copy of the *Abrégé d'astronomie*, by J. Lalande,[59] a volume in-8°; the right principles are set out in a very sensible way; you'll discover that it's the Earth that turns, and the Sun turns only on its own axis. Tell me the names of the ignorant men who are making you learn Ptolemy.

The old proverb that says: 'Tell me who you frequent and I'll tell you who you are' is perfectly correct and deserves to be meditated on and properly understood. Indeed, we understand only those ideas that are close to our own, and we always find those ideas that do not resemble ours ridiculous and hateful. Hence the fact that, since you have ideas that are very different from those of the social circle mentioned, those people strike you as ridiculous. After all, what is the point of wasting such a precious, irrevocable time in playing around and saying silly, false things? You are in your seventeenth year: remember that it is passing and will never return, and that you will reproach yourself, in three years, for every moment you waste talking with people who have only false ideas.

Every man regards the actions of another man as *virtuous*, *vicious* or *permitted*, depending on whether they are *useful*, *harmful* or *indifferent* to him. This moral truth is general and without exception.

You will be able to see, as a consequence of this luminous principle, that men have only ever given the name of *great* to someone who has done them a great service, or greatly amused them. We say 'Henri the Great' when talking of Henri IV, because he made France happy, and the French hope, through the honours they pay to him, that they can encourage kings to follow his example.

People say the Great Homer because, of all poets, he is the one who has given men the most pleasure.

You will note that gratitude is always in proportion with benefits received; hence kings, during their lifetimes, have a great reputation; they die, they can no longer be useful, their reputation decreases every day.

If the poet has depicted nature without any foreign adornments, and if, in consequence, he continues to entertain mankind, his reputation, far from diminishing, increases.

Virgil, at the court of Augustus, was certainly put in the shade by that emperor; nowadays, people talk about Virgil much more than they do about Augustus; in a thousand years' time, people will still be talking about Virgil, and Augustus will be forgotten. You can see why: Virgil's works still give pleasure to those who read them; the small amount of good that Augustus did has long since been destroyed.

Apply this line of reasoning to all great men, and you'll see how true it is that *each man judges everything in accordance with his self-interest.*

Do write longer letters to me, my dear Pauline, the sweetest moments in my life are those when I can talk to you; write your letters several times over, and in particular don't try to be a phrase-maker; there's nothing more laborious than trying to be witty, and eventually people give up on things that are laborious. Indeed, in any kind of thing, woe betide those who *try*; what is done laboriously is never pleasing. That's a whole lot of maxims, but this is because I'd like to get you into the habit of thinking; only commonsense is lasting. The more women I see, the more I feel how wrong they are not to study: I mean to study agreeable things; for boredom is no use at all.

Take my word for it, we can overcome all our failings; we need merely to demonstrate clearly to ourselves that something is necessary, and we will complete it.

I think that not many men are as little disposed to learn languages as myself. However, I realised that I needed to know them, and within two years I'll have a good knowledge of Greek, Latin, English and Italian.

Why are you learning Italian? Obviously to read the fine works of literature written in that language: the *Gerusalemme liberata* is one of the finest. So you need to start it straightaway and get your teacher to explain it to you. Here's how:

I've written the basics of grammar on a separate sheet so that you can show it.[60] Use my method straightaway, and you can be sure that, if your teacher resists it, he's an *impostor* who's teaching you things he doesn't know himself; in that case, he'll be obliged to study the four octaves of Tasso himself, and there's nothing wrong with that. That's how I plan to keep you busy this autumn. […]

H. B.

[1803]

Now that you have become reasonable, I am inviting you to examine in succession everything that you have been taught up until now, and to believe nothing (apart from religion) unless it seems credible to you.

There are several degrees of likelihood. The odds are a hundred million to one that what you have seen actually exists.

The odds are only ten million to one that what Caroline tells you she has seen actually exists.

The odds are ten million to one that Louis XIV existed, but only two million to one that Clovis really lived.

The odds are only eight hundred thousand to one that Ptolemy Philadelphos reigned in Egypt.

The odds are only eight hundred thousand to one that Nimrod existed.

Finally, the odds are even that Neoptolemus taught the Greeks to cultivate wheat and to use it for food instead of eating acorns.

This is the only reasonable way of believing. Examine carefully any man who tells you the opposite. For my part, I am convinced that such a man will have some reason for trying to deceive you.

Everything that one man says to another man can also, on being explained, be brought down to another truth as evident as this one:

Every stick has two ends,

or to a falsity as palpable as the following:

There are sticks that do not have two ends.

We call *virtue* the habit of actions useful to all men; *vice* the habit of actions harmful to all men.

21st Prairial Year XII [10th June 1804]

My dearest, your letter gives me great pain; I'll write to you every two days to take your mind off things. I'm writing to my Papa today to thank him for the two hundred and four francs he has sent me; they could not have come at a better time: for a week I'd been wearing shoes with holes in, and I needed all my wit to slip a little paw dyed black with ink under the hole.

I owe money to the boarding-house where I eat and where I am hardly recognised; I owe money to my porter; I owe money to my tailor, who used to come and see me every morning; my watch has been in hock for a long time now. I haven't been out at all for a fortnight, since I haven't even got twelve *sous* in my pocket; I'm neglecting M. D[aru], G[ener]al M[ichaud], Mlle Duchesnois![61] How many reasons I have to despair!

Well, never have I laughed more: three years ago, I would have despaired; I have become sensible since then. The life of the most powerful man who ever existed, Alexander the Great, and the life of the lowliest bourgeois resemble one another insofar as they are a mixture of a few intense pleasures and many times when, if the man is wise, he is happy; if he is not, he is bored and unhappy.

Boredom is forgivable only when one is your age and has not yet learned to avoid it; later on, the man who gets bored is a fool, a burden on others, and thus is shunned by all.

If you have an ounce of boredom today, your neighbours will notice it and shun you; the next day, you have a pound of it; the day after that, two pounds, and little by little you become stupid.

I've been through all of those states.

Men have various resources against boredom.

First, you need to shift your body when you're bored, that's the surest means. So I often used to go horse riding; I tried to act as a second in duels, to have, in short, something to feel passionate about; with the passions, you are never bored; without them, you are stupid. [...]

I have committed, in Italy and France, follies that might have led to my losing everything, even my honour; for example, I climbed up behind a coach for a whole evening, as a lackey; I have taken a book from a library because I was told that the book was used to conceal letters in. I got away with it all through sheer good luck and a bold frankness inspired in me by passion: right now, the thought makes me shudder.

However, news of it all got out, even the things I never confided to anyone; people said to me that I'd got up behind a coach wearing livery, etc.

There you can see the great difference between a man and a woman! The ten thousandth part of these adventures would have ruined Lucretia herself forever; that's what you need to tell yourself. A man of wit will say to women: Be pretty if you can, be respected since you must; it is said – and it is true – that respect is the opinion of the greatest number; the greatest number is a fool; so should one commit foolish acts? No, but often abstain from doing what is sensible.

I've mentioned you in my letter to Papa; I've asked him to provide you with some entertainment, to let you read some amusing stories, such as *Cleveland*.[62]

Here is some work that will be more useful than anything and I strongly suggest you start it on 26 Prairial; you are to draw up the list of virtues and vices, like this:

Ambition. Intrepidity.
Envy. Patience.
Anger. Magnanimity. (Scaevola burns his hand.
Vertot, chap. XVIII, p. 512)[63]

You must write each of these names at the head of a big sheet (in-4⁰) of paper, and underneath it an abbreviated version of the story, two lines maximum, citing the place where you found it. You can use Rollin's *Histoire romaine*,[64] which is composed of two things: what he translates from the Ancients, which is excellent; what he adds, which is awful. There are about two thirds of his own stuff; skip that, and home in on the rest. After the stories from history, put the fine poetic imitations, for example: anger – Achilles, third book of Homer's *Iliad*, page 412 of the first volume.

This is the most useful kind of work I've managed to find for myself. [...]

Monday, 22nd Prairial Year XII [11th June 1804]

We judge other people to be like ourselves: there is nothing less true, if it's a person of sensibility who is speaking. A passionate young girl hazily imagines that passions govern everyone, whereas out of every hundred people there are eighty-eight whose only passion is vanity (a sense of pride about petty things).

The language of society is deceptive; people pretend to yield to a feeling, when in fact they are merely yielding to a more or less well-calculated interest, and play-acting more or less skilfully.

In what is called good company, there is less hypocrisy: this stems, I believe, from the fact that everybody has read Jean-Jacques, Helvétius, Seneca, Duclos, etc., and has acknowledged that several of their principles are correct.[65]

Fontenelle,[66] the man who affected the greatest subtlety of mind, and his disciple Marivaux, who is a better man than he is, contributed to driving hypocrisy out of the customs and manners of good company.

The man who plunges into social life has to give up living independently; he can no longer exist except through others, but also, others exist only through him.

For example, a fashionable man today (Prairial Year XII) gets up at ten, puts on a frock coat, goes to take a bath and from there to lunch. He comes back home, picks up his boots and a half worn-out suit, and spends his time until half past three making visits, not on business, but to converse with the people he encounters. What about? He doesn't even know himself, when he goes out. He chats about the things people chat about. At four o'clock he comes home, goes out for dinner, comes back, gets dressed, goes out to the theatre from seven until half past nine, leaves after the first play, puts on leather trousers and silk stockings and a triple jabot and goes out to take tea until midnight or one o'clock, staying if he's enjoying himself, and vanishing as soon as the people and things around him start to bore him.

But he is careful to spare the vanity of others, that universal passion; even if he slips off, feeling bored, he pretends to be doing so with the greatest reluctance. When he finds his evenings boring, he goes at 11 pm to Frascati's,[67] a garden where you can eat ices and where you only ever find people of tone. In the whole of this great city of Paris, there are maybe a thousand elegant young men; they all know each other by sight, and even more by the way they dress. A fool can dress well with twenty-five *louis*; but, if I see him from behind, fifty paces ahead of me, I can already say: 'That man does not belong to high society'.

I could write fifty pages on this topic.

'How can one recognise good company?' you will ask me. 'They all think they are good.'

'By the art with which they spare the vanity of others: the more a society seems to be composed of friends who all love and cherish each other, who are extremely witty and yet the most modest people in the world, the more it has tone.'

Deep down, they neither love nor hate one another; on the whole, they are kindly people and have an extreme sense of vanity – one which takes offence at, and delights in, the smallest trifles; but they never show they are upset. Anyone who shows in public (in the eyes of society) that he is upset about something is a fool, or a man filled with pride.

If he thinks anyone else shares his sorrows, he's a fool; if he thinks himself important enough to inflict them on you, he's too proud.

It's not possible to describe an agreeable man in a letter: you have to see several of them at a time to judge them, since only an agreeable man will let himself be drawn into trying to excel, and thereby commits the greatest fault imaginable; he offends the vanity of all those who are present, starting with all the men he has outshone, and followed by all the women to whom he does not speak. It's easier to say what the agreeable man *mustn't* be like.

Society is growing more perfect every day, since people are learning to provide it with better amusement: an agreeable man from the days of Louis XIV, Lauzun, Matta, the Chevalier de Gramont,[68] etc., who have all left such a fine reputation behind, would seem as dull and ponderous as anything these days, reeling out their compliments by the yard.

The people we find agreeable these days would doubtless have the same defect in a hundred years if they were to awaken, like Epimenides.[69]

It is so difficult to understand society! For this reason, you can't learn anything about it from books; on the contrary, the more you read, the more you ruin your sense of judgment. You need to reason properly, and then six months' experience and good advice will form your character. There is, however, one book that's useful because it's a model of conversation: La Bruyère.

Farewell, my dearest; I wanted to write a few sentences for tomorrow's letter, and I've let myself get carried away. Try, each day, to understand my letters; they'll entertain you.

You asked me what 'finesse' means.

It's the habit of using terms that leave a great deal to be guessed at – in such a way that a man from the provinces who turned up wouldn't understand a thing – or perhaps the opposite of what was really meant.

18th Messidor Year XII [7th July 1804]

[…] While we're on the subject of English, my Papa says you want to learn it: I only wish I could hand over to you what I know; those English are gloomy, commonsensical people; I don't know of any people more talkative and yet more frigid. They have only ever produced one great man and one madman. The great man is Shakespeare; the madman, Milton. There are only a few good bits in the latter, and M. Letourneur has provided us with an excellent translation of the first, a man with the divine spark.

Do learn Italian. 'But there aren't any teachers'. So learn it by yourself. Learn that wonderful language in which you can find Dante, Boccaccio, Ariosto, Tasso, Alfieri, Goldoni, Metastasio, Machiavelli and so many others. Of all these writers, only Dante and Boccaccio are passably translated; and even Rivarol has only translated a third of the sublime Dante. Look up the story of Ugolino in canto XXXIII; that is the most terrifying poetry in existence: there is nothing to match it even in the sublime Homer. This is the sublime in the *genus* 'terrifying'; work out what that canto means by looking up every word in the dictionary. You can be sure that you won't find in the English (with the exception of Shakespeare and Milton) a single line of verse as fine as the ninety lines of that sublime passage. Hurry up and learn Italian: it's a language full of gaiety; I've never found any gaiety in English except in *Henry V*, one of Shakespeare's plays; but with a book by Boccaccio, Ariosto or Goldoni, you have to stop reading if you don't want to die of laughter. You need to read plays written in Tuscan; for example, *Il Cavaliere di buon gusto*, *La Donna di Garbo*, *Il Moliere*. You'll find in *Il Cavaliere di buon gusto* and *La Donna di Garbo* examples to follow.[70]

I've finally discovered what counts as 'ridiculous':

We call 'ridiculous' the actions of a man who aims at the same happiness as us, and who takes the wrong path, because he lacks something that we have and that we do not think we are capable of losing as we strive for the same happiness; and yet everyone uses the word 'ridiculous': but they are not giving a definition of the word, just an example of its use [***]

20th Thermidor Year XII [8th August 1804]

[…] I'm reconciled with the world; I see from afar societies composed of superior men and women; there are almost no errors in circulation in those societies; they are soil that has been well tilled for happiness; it is up to you to sow it with good seed; but I had to travel far and wide before finding this well-tilled soil!

People who are happy know, if they are witty, that the vast majority of men are sunk in boredom, and only escape it by the passion of envy; so they conceal their lives; that's their secret. We who have the inestimble happiness of being passionate must try to uproot the passions that we will probably not be able to satisfy, so as to kindle, on the contrary, those that we will be able to satisfy, and we shall be very happy; but the passport into these social circles is a great deal of wit, in other words a *head* full of *truths*, most of them on the ordinary subjects of conversation, namely man and his passions.

So let us observe; this merely increases the sensibility of our souls, and without sensibility, there is no happiness.

Jean-Jacques had been bored in society, and he had led me to look on it with a jaundiced eye; but now I'm cured of my bad temper. Read that great man; but remember that he was always in a bad mood. Tell me what you're reading; and send me four or five character sketches of women, I'd really appreciate that; write to me more often. And what the devil are you getting up to? Falling in love? You're crazy! Make sure you don't marry for love; unless you marry a man with a great deal of wit, you won't be happy. If I were you, I'd take an honest gentleman, very well-off, less witty than you are. Actually, that's also what Mlle de M… thinks.

3rd Fructidor Year XII [21st August 1804]

I could really do with you here, my dear Pauline: there are times when the soul is heartily tired of work and strives to love, attaching itself more and more to the objects of its affection, in which it takes shelter and near which it would like to remain for anything in the whole world. For several days I have been overwhelmed by this feeling that returns all too often for my peace of mind. As long as the soul is frigid, or not greatly agitated, Paris is the best city to be; but as soon as the soul becomes tender again, I miss Grenoble, however boring it might be. Why can't I see you here with another person? How happy I would be to be able to spend the evenings in your company, far from all the intrigues and all the cares of the world! Why can't I gather around myself a family of the kind I imagine must exist? I fear that we don't enjoy this pleasure in our youth; so we will spend the time for love without fully enjoying its happiness, and it will be only when our soul is enfeebled and capable of only feeble sensations, and our aged heads will have become set in their ways, that we'll be able to live together.

I'll let you into a great secret: today, 3rd Fructidor, I have started to take lessons in declamation from Larive, a famous tragic actor.[71] It's not that I'm getting particularly into this art just yet; but the doctors have advised me to find an occupation to take my mind off things; they told me I would die of melancholy if I didn't follow their advice. I go with Martial Daru; from now on we'll call him Pacé. So I went along this morning; I came back at eleven to work, but I couldn't settle down to anything; I needed to be with people I love, to talk to them, to hug them to my chest, and not to work at discovering new truths. I picked up some novels, and they all struck me as silly and overblown, rather than tender; I tried to read *La Nouvelle Héloïse*; but I already know it off by heart. So I spent the whole day dreaming, and now I'm off to the theatre for a change of scene. It's not that the state in which I find myself, this over-abundance of tenderness, is painful; it would be happiness itself if one had someone to say 'I love you!' to, but the only people I can find here are men of wit or else half-donkeys. All the little girls in these parts bore me; their tenderness is merely insipid flirtatiousness, affected airs and graces; there's nothing absolutely frank, natural, energetic. Everything I love is in Grenoble or eighty leagues away from here; I can write only to you, the other person has perhaps forgotten me: that's what makes me melancholy. I've finally dreamt up a way of writing to her; but whatever will she think of my letter? Will she reply? Isn't she maybe in love with another man? I've had a wonderfully crazy idea: before returning to Grenoble, I'll go incognito to the town where she is, and there revel in the pleasure of seeing her. It's a pretty fantastic idea, but it will give me pleasure and won't harm anyone; I don't see why I shouldn't just go ahead and do it. I'll start saving up for the trip soon: she'd be so surprised if she went out for a walk through the park in the evening and, at nightfall, spotted me between the trees.

What are you doing in Grenoble? Are the pre-supper gatherings still as boring? And what about you? Give me lots of details about your life; do you see much of the M… girls? Bear in mind that love is something divine, except when it determines who you marry; thousands of examples convince me of this every day; the only real marriages are marriages of convenience. If that weren't the case, I'd be married already.

If you want my opinion, our friend A [***] seems to suit you down to the ground. Any news on this score? On the trip to [***] he was half in thrall to your beauty.

From Pauline Beyle[72]

Grenoble, Sunday 8th Fructidor Year XII [26th August 1804]

My good Henri,

   You've received yesterday's letter from me. Right now, my head is a little calmer. I think my letter was full of nonsense. I was almost sorry I'd sent it; it must have irritated you, but you were astonished at my silence. I'd already written five or six letters, then I threw them on the fire. I kept telling you the same things. I'll give you an account of how I spend my day. You'll see what fun I'm having. I get up at 5 or half 5; at ¼ to 6 I have my drawing lesson until half 6; from half 6 to half 8, when M. David arrives, I study mat[hs]. At 9, we have lunch; when my f[ather] is in G[renoble], he never stops talking about his speculations in agriculture or building. When I can in all decency get away before 10, I do some reading to shake off my boredom, since I'm already bored. At 11 until half 11 I practise or have my piano lesson; then I read until 2. At 3 I read a bit more to rid my head of all the nonsense I've heard during lunch. When my f[ather] isn't there, as often happens just now, the conversation is always about sermons, priests, masses. I can imagine that such things might interest them, but when it comes to the cooks, the servant girls, the events in the rue Vieux-J[ésuites], I have no idea what they can see in any of that. From 4 until night time, I draw, I read, and then I go to my grandfather's. I'm glad when he stays to play cards, as he always does ever since he had pneumonia. Then I go for a walk by myself; I can think about you, wish I was with you. If only I could see you for one hour every evening, I'd forget what a boring day it was. When the card game breaks up, I go to see my auntie and usually have to attend the sermons that my auntie or grandfather preach to me, since I never know what they're saying. Once upon a time I used to pretend I was paying attention, and sometimes made up some questions to ask them. Since I realised this was a waste of time, I think of other things. I retire at half 10, after putting up with another sermon. They claim I have no sensibility and do not love them, because I retire early; but at that time of the day I go to bed to forget the boredom of the day. Such is my day, my dear friend. I'm 18 and 1/4; I've lived in this never-ending boredom for several years. For the last few years I kept hoping it would end. This gave me courage to put up with it, but now I have lost all hope; life is a burden to me, if it never changes. During the two hours I spend at auntie's, you can't imagine the number of absurd things I hear being said; you just can't imagine; such weird stories. A while ago, I took your advice and wrote down part of what I heard, but I'm so bored that I can't go on. […]

11th Fructidor Year XII [29th August 1804]

Your letter alarms me more than I can possibly say.[73] You're about to commit an act of madness. Just remember that going to Voreppe without your father's permission lowers you forever from the status you may have in the world, and places you in the ranks of fallen women.[74]

That's the truth, on my soul and conscience. I swear that I'll never let on. Remember that from where you are, you can see only the good sides of a life of wandering. You don't take into account all its discomforts. One of these days you're going to receive a letter that will be the best reply to that of the 5th. In it, you'll see how one can sometimes feel sad at one's isolation, and then, think of the difference between you and me.

As a man, I have a heart that is three or four times less sensitive, because I have three or four times more good sense and experience of the world – what you women call hardness of heart.

As a man, I have the opportunity to have mistresses. The more I have and the greater the scandal, the more reputation and brilliance I enjoy in society. I left Grenoble at the age of seventeen; I am now twenty-one; in the meantime I've had as many women as anyone could have; well, two years ago, I was already starting to feel jaded with that kind of life. So much so that, in spite of being twenty-one, and despite my fortunate position of not having an income of even twelve francs per year, I'd marry another Pauline if I could find one who wasn't my sister, even if it meant earning a living as something, a printer for instance, a newspaper hack or something even more dismal.

Since you have a much more tender soul and haven't grown jaded after four years living out in society, before two years you'd be ardently longing to meet an agreeable man. You'd desire him so intensely that

44

you'd end up persuading yourself (like Mary Wollstonecraft Godwin, the famous Englishwoman) that you've found him, and this would be far from the case. By dint of desiring something, in this category where illusion is so easy, you finally persuade yourself that the thing is actually true. *And the irreparable failing of having made a mistake deprives one forever of the possibility of having a worthy husband.*

Remember this truth: who would wish – even if he were in love with her – to marry a girl who'd run away from her parents' home?

I am the least prejudiced man I have ever met, and I can assure you that I wouldn't do it. If I loved her, I'd *beat* her, and then I'd dump her.

Remember that, in society, you won't find twenty souls that understand yours; I've acquired twenty times more experiences than you ever could, and I haven't even found *four*. Think about that number. One of them is Mlle Victorine Bigillion,[75] who's just done exactly the same as you would like to do. She lived alone in Saint-Ismier; this increased the strength of her passions and her intelligence. She has such great intelligence that her father decided she was *mad*. Thereupon, she was locked away practically as if she *were* mad; the poor girl was driven to extremities; she escaped to Moirans; they caught up with her, and she is at present, I believe, in prison at the Grande-Chartreuse where she'll stay as long as her parents, whom she has insulted in every way, wish. The only way she could get out would be if she married, and who'd want anything to do with her?

That's the truth about this episode. Try to get someone to relate the story to you, and you'll see how the public judges people with any strength of soul. If it could see them as they really are, it would simply be jealous of them; but it doesn't understand them and thinks they're mad.

Never was an example closer to you than this same poor Victorine.

In Italy, I knew a woman called Angelina;[76] I loved her more than words can tell. She had exactly the same character as you. She spent her youth without committing any follies – she spent that time shut away (or at least for two years) in a convent, forced to live there. She eventually got married and for eight years she's been the happiest of women.

Remember that Saint-Preux[77] is an imaginary character, as are all the heroes in novels. Read Molière, La Bruyère, history: that's what man is like. [...]

In society, my dearest, you will find a great number of dry souls: those are people who have never in all their lives had a moment of sadness, of that unctuous sadness that we have often felt; they are usually susceptible to only two passions, vanity and the love of money. That dryness comes from the soul. The rest of us are sensitive souls; we often weep at an idea that passes through our heads. I've just been out to buy this writing paper; I went down a street called the Rue des Orties – a rather apt name, since nobody goes down it;[78] on one side it is lined by the majestic gallery of the Museum. This gallery rises very high and is very black; the street is narrow and silent, and there are very tall houses opposite. Here I encountered a woman of forty, aged and poverty-stricken, carrying her child behind her and singing for alms. This, together with the aspect of the street – which had already had an impact on me – touched me. As I listened more closely, I heard her singing a song of the Guards; that wrought my heart and brought tears to my eyes. I walked more quickly, and only when I was on the Pont-Royal did I realise I hadn't given her anything. There are so many impoverished charlatans in Paris that it's necessary, if you're not very wealthy yourself, not to keep giving. However, I was deeply sorry that I hadn't given anything to that poor mother. Then I reflected that her song had brought the tears to my eyes because I could see that the words, which were coarse and vulgar, must be destroying, in the hearts of her listeners, the very feeling from which she was hoping to draw some charity. Every mother, on seeing her pass by with her child on her back, was filled with pity, and said to herself, 'One day, I might be reduced to that extremity'. But on hearing her song, the pity evaporated: 'I'll never lead a depraved life; that woman does, no doubt, her song proves as much, and it must be her depraved life that has brought her to this'.

Notice how much the *head* influences the *heart*: a thousand people in Paris might pass that way and have the same feelings; there are perhaps not four who would have analysed those feelings. Many wouldn't have been able; most of them, indeed, would have shaken off that importunate image. Here you can see, in second place, the influence of the *head* on the *heart*; that woman wished for charity, she put on a good act, she had had the right idea in carrying her child on her back, but she'd chosen the wrong song; she should have gone for a sad romance; so this was a failure of intelligence paralysing all the rest. [...]

13th Nivose Year XIII [3rd January 1805]

While I was reading this evening, my dear Pauline, the *Confessions* of Jean-Jacques[79], not for the facts but for the style, as a practised ear enjoys recognising *divinamente suave d'un instrumento*,[80] I found, on p. 135, vol. II, that when he first squared a binomial and then found that this square was equal to the square of the first term plus twice the product of the first and second terms plus the square of the second term, he thought he'd made a mistake, and continued to think so until a diagram had resolved his doubt.[81]

I was amazed to think I'd never really grasped that, since I have studied mathematics and loved it so ardently; but it strikes me that we really only grasp things with maturity; this is a useful habit, you should acquire it early; so I amused myself by drawing the diagram and describing it on blank pages that I've had inserted at the end of each bound volume, and it occurred to me to write it down for you.[82]

This evening, while strolling down the wooden galleries of the Palais-Royal, I noticed that they were partly in stone. Mante[83] was astonished; I hadn't seen that, despite going for a walk there at least once every two days for three years now. I could have sworn that the whole thing was covered in wood; one should only swear about things one has examined; I might have lost a significant bet on this question.

Rousseau's second walk, the story of him being knocked over by the Great Dane,[84] is a masterpiece of style, it has the same impression on me as the sublime aria *del Matrimonio segreto*, Cimarosa:

Ah! Pietade troveremo
Se il ciel barbaro non é[85]

when it is sung well, i.e. it gives me a wonderful sense of happiness.

These are two pleasures that Jean has no idea of; the benefits of education; but how many pains there are that he doesn't feel and that we do! However, I think that, for a soul that has managed to extirpate all the vices, and contrived to acquire the habit of justice, the state of culture is by far the happiest, because of the fine arts and the sciences, but the fine arts above all: painting, poetry, representation, sculpture, architecture.

29th Germinal Year XIII [19th April 1805]

This morning, I needed the pleasures of tenderness and intimacy; I reread your letters, they filled me with delight, especially one dated 9th Messidor where you're even earlier than usual; admittedly, you felt obliged to apologise for this the next day, since you were afraid *it might have annoyed me*. A fine thing to be afraid of! You are destined, my Pauline, to become an extraordinary woman. There's one thing that gives birth to great genius: melancholy. A great soul who *conceives* of the joys of heaven imagines they might appear in one's lifetime, and still waits for them afterwards, on seeing that they do not in fact materialise. In other words, dry and frigid souls – the vast majority of people – can neither share these transports of delight nor give them back in return. Our great soul is filled with unhappiness and says to itself 'I deserved better!' And the sweet tears of melancholy spring to its eyes. Then these pleasures acquire an additional charm because one regrets being unable to encounter them; we dwell on them in detail so as to console ourselves, and thereby become capable of depicting them. That was the experience of Jean-Jacques, Racine, Shakespeare, Virgil, etc., and all the great geniuses who were *men of sensibility*. When they were also men of intelligence, and knew what true virtue was, like Homer and Corneille, they managed to produce the finest works of art known to mankind. Imagine a tragedy in which there would be a role for Hermione or Phèdre, and in which the men would be Horace, or Cinna, or Sévère. The human heart wouldn't be able to cope with so many beauties if they were well acted; everyone would be finding it difficult to breathe in the third act and would have to leave with a vile headache by the fourth. […]

All the great *sensitive* painters also started with *melancholy*; this is the feeling inspired by Raphael's heads and Poussin's landscapes. When you're well-disposed, indeed, they produce the most complete illusion, the illusion which least needs any help from us; but often, almost always, their works are spoiled by one's true knowledge of true virtue. What a picture Raphael would have painted if, instead of painting insipid trash such as those everlasting *Holy Families*, he'd painted Tancredi recognising his mistress after just killing her! Any man of genius sensitive to painting must find this the finest subject in existence, just as for a *sublime* genius (or one drawn to scenes of terror) the finest subject is Jupiter blasting the Giants with a thunderbolt. This latter theme is treated quite well by Giuliano Romano, in the Palazzo Té in Mantua: as for the first, I've only ever seen a wretched daub in the local museum.

All famous women started out being melancholy, like you; Mme Roland, for instance.[86] The Empress of Russia,[87] who dethroned her husband, owed all her genius to the prison she spent time in, to French books and to the friendship of Princess Kurakin.[88] Read Rulhière.[89]

This fate for women is much commoner in the world than is usually thought, since women have no direct action on our behaviour and can act only by impelling others to act. How many unhappy women perish of languor, since nobody can help them, and the barbarians who kill them don't even realise what they are doing.

The tragedy of sensitive souls is that they explain the words of dry people in their own way. The latter tell us that the main thing to possess is one's freedom. That may be true for them, but not exactly for us; a certain degree of freedom is necessary, since without it, everything turns to poison; but absolute freedom is isolation, and this imperils the life of States. Look at the eighty-year-old beggar who stints himself of half his loaf to feed his little dog.

A thousand things that slide over their dry souls and that they don't even notice constitute the happiness or unhappiness of a tender soul, and most of the things that we envy because the *dries* tell us we should are not even pleasures for us – all the delights of vanity, for example. A soul like yours, my dear Pauline, draws more pleasure from a beautiful tree that it comes across while out for a walk than they derive from a superb, brand-new coach and horses in which they hope to cut a brilliant figure; they can see that, in general, they seem much less brilliant than they had expected, while you can sit under your tree and imagine lovers filled with happiness, husbands and wives taking their two-year-old toddler out for a walk, Sappho filling the forests with her accents sublime, and the thousands and thousands of pictures that your imagination has provided your heart with.

You should try to make as many of these pictures as possible become realities in your life; with this in mind, you should study the world you live in and ensure that your heart doesn't delude you by showing you things that don't exist. […]

Happiness consists in being able to satisfy our passions, so long as we have only happy passions. Hatred, vanity, cruelty, for example, are passions that, generally speaking, give more unhappiness than happiness. We can believe the opposite to be true of friendship, love, the love of glory, that of our native land, etc. […]

This study[90] is disagreeable; but it's by dissecting those who have died in hospital, often from contagious diseases, that the doctor learns how to save that alluring beauty whom a stomach abscess was about to carry off from her parents and her distraught lover the day before their wedding. It's excellent that boredom is forcing you to undertake this disgusting and necessary study. That's why young Parisians who are never bored at sixteen are so stupid, so bored, and so boring at twenty-six;[91] that's the radical vice of Parisian households. So write some character studies of the illustrious figures who are playing the game; imagine that a tribunal composed of Shakespeare, Helvétius, Montaigne, Molière, and Jean-Jacques asks you for a description of M. X… What will you reply? […]

Marseille, 2nd Fructidor Year XIII [20th August 1805]

Your letter is delightful for me, my dear Pauline, and for anyone else it would be sublime. What gives me most delight is its natural, profound depiction of a sublime and touching character. And that's exactly what you wanted to take out.[92] So stop making that error of judgement that makes you believe that the least interesting parts in your letters are the ones where you talk about yourself. It's an excessive modesty that leads you into that error. Firstly for me, you know those are the most interesting. For the public, if your letters were destined to be published, they would still be the most interesting parts – they show a great character, together with a profound sensibility, and that is what is most touching.

The rest of your letters would be interesting only insofar as they would contain something of yourself – well, the merely narrative part would generally not be of great account to the public, since chance has not yet made you a witness of particularly interesting events. The deeper one digs into one's soul, the more emboldened one is to express a more secret thought, and the more one trembles when it is written down: the thought appears strange, and this strangeness is what constitutes its merit. That's why it is original, and if it is also true, if your words copy what you feel accurately, it is sublime. So write to me exactly what you feel.

There's a potential reef looming for those who adopt this habit. We don't feel intelligent enough to depict just what we are thinking, and, though we agree in principle, we behave as if we didn't believe it. This is wrong: we need to write at every moment, not just at some. For example, I was never less in a mood to write as at this very moment. I've been working like a devil all morning, copying out letters that are a pig's breakfast when it comes to their thought – and for their style. Then I read a horribly overblown book[93] (i..e the expressions in it exaggerate the thoughts and feelings of the author). This failing is the worst of all, in my view; it's the one that keeps sensibility most at bay. We should write only when we have great or deeply-felt things to say, but then we need to say them with the utmost simplicity. As if we were taking pains to prevent them from being noticed. This is the opposite of what the fools of this day and age do, but all great men have acted thus. […]

Marseille, 9th Fructidor Year XIII [27th August 1805]

On Sunday, St Louis's Day, 1805, we[94] went into the country: I'll remember this day out my whole life long. The Marseille region is dry and arid; it hurts the eyes, being so ugly. The air hurts the lungs with its extreme dryness. Clouds of dust stop the horses from trotting and suffocate the travellers. The only trees are horrid little willows, clogged with dust; these little willows are actually olive trees, and they are so precious that the locals say: He who has ten thousand olive trees can make ten thousand *écus* from them. There are indeed a few trees like those on the Cours[95], at Grenoble; but their leaves are always white with powder, and half unfurled because of the extreme heat; and far from giving pleasure, the shade they are in makes one feel sorry for the suffering they endure, and you wish on their behalf that they had been born in the forest of Fontainebleau.

One league to the east of Marseille there is a little valley formed by two rows of completely dry rocks; in the whole chain, you wouldn't find a blade of greenery in a space as big as this great sheet of paper. Just a few sprigs of lavender, mint, balm – but these are not green and, from a few steps away, indistinguishable from the grey of the rock. At the far end of the valley there's a river as big as the *robine*,[96] called the Huveaune. This river enlivens a half-league of terrain called the Pomone, because it is filled with apple-trees.

The Huveaune flows along one side of the port. It's surrounded by tall trees and, under these trees, charming little pathways, and every now and again benches dotted around amid the greenery, it's just as green and fresh as Cheylas.[97] Anywhere else, it would be merely beautiful; here, the contrast makes it magical. There's a castle with high towers, but surrounded by such a thick clump of chestnut trees that only the tops of the towers can be seen above the trees. This castle really looks like some fairyland sojourn; just imagine those towers, from some tale of chivalry, emerging from the superb chestnut trees. Leading to this castle, which inspires one with thoughts that are not sombre (the towers are not thick or dark enough) but melancholy, they've laid out a pretty little avenue of plane trees – maybe five or six years old, and as thick as the smallest of the cherry trees among the limes. Their cheerful greenery makes a deep contrast with the castle and the tall chestnuts.

I thought I was hearing a piece by Cimarosa in which that great master of the heart's emotions, among some grand and terrible arias in the middle of some sublime work, vigorously depicting all the horrors of vengeance, jealousy and unrequited love, has set a pretty little melody with an accompaniment for the *musette*. In this way, cheerfulness is found next to the profoundest sorrow. I've just heard a young girl singing a cheerful song; perhaps her sister back home had just poisoned herself out of despair and was breathing her last. So reflects the man who listens to this sublime work, if he is worthy of hearing it and understanding the little tune. That is how artists ask to be understood. That is how we are affected by the little avenue of plane trees or syca-mores, those trees with a pretty nankeen-type bark, leaves like those of the vine and, as fruits, prickly chestnuts dangling from a long tail. You find some in the first fifty trees of the Cours at La Graille.

We'd brought along a brace of partridge and a roast pigeon, a pie, a fricandeau,[98] some peaches, grapes and a bottle of Bordeaux. We set off at three; we stopped at a small inn that we cherished because of you. Twenty-five days ago, on our way to the Pomone, or rather on our way home from it, I went into this inn to ask for lemonade or wine. Next to the door, I found a pretty four-year-old boy who was sleeping in the position of one of the figures of the Infant Jesus as painted by Raphael. He had a face out of Greuze, thanks to his lovely black eyes and his blond hair that fell in thick curls across his shoulders. I showed him to her; she found him charming. But she remarked that there was something a little strange about his physiognomy: his face, especially his pose, expressed a serene and tranquil repose; his eyes expressed sorrow. We made inquiries: they had just set his leg – he had broken it two hours previously. [...]

From Pauline Beyle

Wednesday [4th September 1805]

My dear friend,

You must have received my letter of credit. It left here several days ago. I showed my grandfather your last letter. Your linen was sent off on Monday. Except for good old Auntie G[agnon], they're all hard-hearted. The day before yesterday we were having dinner at grandfather's. I'd just received your letter; as I came back into the living room, I found everyone busy admiring my Papa's tenderness for his children. Grandfather was saying that he sacrificed all of his own pleasures so that we would be rich one day, and my f[ather] was acting all modest. This sight filled me with indignation. I had your letter in the bosom of my dress; I was quite prepared to read from it the proof of his love for you.[99] I couldn't stand it any longer; I went out onto the terrace; my grandfather followed me out; I handed him your letter and left his house. But anyway, my friend, let's not say any more about it. From you, I have a thousand proofs of their hardness of heart. I'll write to you often. Don't have any worries about me; when I can't stay in Grenoble any longer, I go to Claix. Since you left, I've made a charming discovery; maybe you know the waterfall at Allières; there's no need to give you a description of it. I spend my whole life there; I just can't tell you how much pleasure I get out of reading Shakespeare or Ossian in this tranquil spot. I still haven't seen anyone here. M. Bigillion is so kind, he often brings me books; he's so thoughtful that I don't know how to thank him. Since my letters don't bore you, when I'm in Claix I'll write down all my thoughts for you; here. I'm not free. If you only knew how much I desire to know Mme L[ouason];[100] how happy I would be to be able to live with her all my life long! The people all around me lead me to think that this would be a happiness beyond price. I was seeking a friend from among my female cousins, yesterday I was at theirs; Mlle Amélie Pasqual has been in Voiron for a few days. She's just come from Paris, where she's spent a year; my c[ousins] were expressing to me their annoyance that my f[ather] wasn't in Grenoble. 'It's all the more irritating,' added one of them, 'because we have ten dresses to make, and we've been putting this off for 2 months, since we're waiting for the new designs that Amélie's bringing from Paris'. This confidential remark left me thunderstruck; I'd never doubted their friendship for their female cousins. So that's the way they love. Farewell, my sole friend. Write to me often. Don't worry about me, for when I'm at Claix, all the silly nonsense that makes me so sad here just makes me laugh. Three days ago I went to an Anacreontic session[101] where I laughed with all my heart. I'd never seen anything so funny in all my life. M. Morel, the president of that august assembly, started by reading us in a pedantic tone of voice a masterpiece of his own fashioning, in which he modestly proved to us that old Corneille was not his equal. Farewell. The bells are chiming midday.

I'm afraid you might be bored, my dearest, and I'm sorry you can't be bothered to tell me about it. Why don't you ever write? I deserve better. […]

Anyway, you're not going to convince me that you don't have any thoughts; whether they are sad or cheerful, your day is made up of a succession of ideas, or simple sensations, or memories, or judgements, or desires; you cannot live without thinking. Even when you're in a state of despair, you're still thinking. Well, I wish you'd share your thoughts with me. They are your essential self, and since your happiness is mine, I need to know you perfectly.

If I weren't already madly in love with another woman, I'd have to conclude, from the regret I feel at the fact you don't write to me, that I was in love with you. Anyway, that beautiful soul, seeing how glum I was at your silence, felt a twinge of jealousy. […]

I am happy here, my dearest, I am tenderly loved by a woman I love to distraction.[102] She has a beautiful soul; no, beautiful isn't the word – sublime! To my chagrin I sometimes even feel jealous. I have studied the passion enough to make me suspicious, since I can see all the things that might possibly happen. Since she's less wealthy than you are and in fact hardly has a penny to her name, I'm going to buy a sheet of official paper to write my testament and leave everything to her and, after her, to my daughter.[103] I don't suppose I've got much; but anyway, I'll have done everything I can. If all of this comes to nothing, and I die, and one day you are rich, I commend this tender soul to you; her only defect is that she is easily overwhelmed by unhappiness. You know this failing from your own experience; you know how greatly a sensitive soul who takes pity on you can be a source of consolation! So, even if you're not rich, you can shed a tear over my ashes by giving your tender friendship to M.G. and my daughter. […]

From Pauline Beyle

Thursday [5th December 1805]

It's one o'clock; the moonlight is superb; for a few days it has been snowing heavily, everything is peaceful around me. This calm is interrupted only by the sound of the fountain and the voice of a few distant dogs. I've resolved to write to you tonight; I won't be interrupted. My soul is as tranquil as everything around me. Ah, my friend, I had been suffering for so long! Let's say no more about it. My dear Henri, you thought I no longer loved you and I didn't have the strength to tell you that you were wrong. I love you just as much as ever, and if I didn't have you at least to love, what would I do in this world? […]

I would however like to give you a reason for my silence. My friend, I have none. I am in a state of such profound ennui that I am doing hardly anything. For four days, I've been swearing to myself that I'd emerge from this lethargy one way or another. I have the choice between a pistol, or reading; my friend, how deeply I feel those lines by André Chénier![104] Twenty times over, as I took up the pistols, I felt a violent desire to discharge them into my heart. I would deliver myself from the burden that oppresses me. I am surrounded by dry souls that are killing me. For two months, I've been forced to live with such stupid, vain people; at any other time I'd just have laughed it off, but right now, it's killing me. […]

I have three volumes of Shakespeare belonging to M. Bigillion that I still haven't given back to him. Since I'm here for just a few days, I won't be here if he comes back. Couldn't I send them to his home address? I still don't have the *Idéologie*. You'd give me great pleasure if you could send me the *Logique*, but only when you don't need it any more.[105] […]

Man means 'homme' in French; *King*, 'roi'; but those words teach you nothing about what man/'homme' is; or in general what a king is, and in particular such-and-such a king. Several, my dear, embrace the study of languages out of laziness (such as Locke).[106] Everything tells them that their happiness requires them to study, but at the same time they find it extremely difficult to think.

Was Frederick II great through the usefulness of his actions, or simply because of their difficulty?

Could anyone have done any better? Did he see what was better and refuse to move it? Or didn't he see it?

Was the corruption of the Regency[107] useful in that it showed up the vileness of despotism?

Have academies spread true enlightenment, have they been useful to the happiness of the majority of mankind?

The solution to such questions, which require thousands of correct judgements, *is intolerable to them*, they find it much less bothersome to get it into their heads that

of man first disobedience and the fruit of that forbiden
de hom[me] première désobéissance et le fruit de ce défendu
tree, single heavenly muse.
arbre chante céleste muse.

mean the words underneath.[108]

This would appear contemptible to them for Latin. Voltaire and his century poured scorn on that craze for Latin but, as apostles of liberty, they started to sing the praises of England in every way. Everybody learned English, and I've seen all those *anglomanes* waxing enthusiastic for *The Rape of the Lock*, a bad little poem by Pope, when they haven't read Boileau's *Le Lutrin*[109] which is worth a whole *perruque* made of those locks. They prefer Shakespeare to Corneille; but if those great geniuses had changed language, they'd have preferred, for the same good reasons, Corneille to Shakespeare.

Guard against making the same ridiculous mistake, my dear. You can esteem the power, the imagination, the truth with which English writers depict nature, but don't let yourself be seduced by their overblown, gigantesque style, their blackness of imagination. Hurry up and study the *Iliad of Pope*, that you haven't sent me, by the way. Few women have read Homer as that great poet deserves to be read, the stop-start phrases of Bitaubé communicate him to them hardly any better than the flaccid lines of Rochefort.[110]

Marseille, Saturday, 22nd March 1806

[…] Let's write to one another, my dear: we are each other's best friend. I love you with all my soul, I will never love any mistress as much as you. When we are both tired of the world, we'll take a small house in Paris or environs, where we will spend our lives together and await our end in the bosom of the fine arts and the most tender friendship. I'm getting carried away in an access of sensibility. I'll break off my letter until tomorrow morning. Farewell. […]

While trying to find some more paper to continue my letter on, I found between two pieces of wood in my desk several letters from a woman, apparently addressed to the man who occupied this room before me… They all bear the mark of petty souls profoundly preoccupied by silly nonsense and affecting little affairs of vanity. They all think themselves to be the unhappiest people in the world, in particular a little girl living with her family in Paris; she's quite well-off and she writes that she's unhappy because people aren't paying her enough attention.

This made me think, for what else is there to do when one is sad and has no means of distraction? We need to make ourselves skilled in the art of happiness. I've seen all men thinking themselves more or less extremely unhappy. Yesterday, three persons (including [***]) told me in confidence that they were the *unhappiest people in the world*. Those are their own terms; the good thing is that they aren't lying; as they think they are unhappy, they repel all the little pleasures that fill up life and become so, soon they are sad, boring, and society lets them get on with it. […]

Supposing that you don't achieve happiness (a state free of pain, the only thing one can procure for oneself), you need to become accustomed early on to bear sorrows, influence yourself, make yourself wise. This is what I was explaining in another letter.

Here are the habits I'm trying to acquire:

1. Exercise, or in ten years fat and gormless.
2. The talent of comicking the hateful and the boring.
3. Choose a job, and get used to it. For this, listen closely to find out what is the dominant passion, so as not to change jobs once they've been chosen.
4. Bearing sorrows.
5. Don't make too much of the happiness you don't enjoy – [***] is unhappy not to be in my place, and vice versa.
6. When you approach a man: What does he need? and not: What do I feel?
7. Habit of sobriety. Study the kinds of food that do us good and get used to them.

Reread this often and write to tell me what you think of this letter. […]

Metz, Saturday 18th October 1806, 2 o'clock

My dear, we left Paris on the 16th at three minutes past six p.m. This is the first moment we have been free to write. We felt rather gloomy as we left Paris. We concluded that we needed to laugh more than ever.

I'm perfectly happy with the way M[artial] is treating me. A big hug from me to you and the whole family.

You've probably heard about the death of Prince Ferdinand.[111] We are going to Cobourg, but the Emperor is doubtless well in advance. We are going on from here to Mainz, from Mainz to Würzburg, from Würzburg to Bamberg, from there to Cobourg and from there on to glory.

Write to me often, please! You can see that my first free moments are devoted to you. I don't have time to repeat to you everything I said in my last letter, but I think it all the more.

A little patience. My fate is probably about to change. This will put me in a position where I can help you out. [...]

[Munnerstadt, October 1806]

My dear,

We slept – for the first time since Paris – in Munnerstadt. We don't have a second to ourselves. We are the first Frenchmen to penetrate this part of the country, which means we need to take a few precautions. If you want to follow the forward march of a heart in which you are always present, look on the map: Metz, Homburg, Mainz, Frankfurt-am-Main. We left this lovely river only yesterday, from Frankfurt to Hanau. A strange adventure – I'll tell you about it. From Hanau to Aschaffenburg; from there to Würzburg; from Würzburg to Werneck and finally Munnerstadt, after fifteen leagues travelled partly on foot in the midst of a storm, with our terrified horses trying to throw us at every moment. At the height of the storm, with water trickling down from my hat into my shirt and my boots, I kept thinking of you. This storm, at half past six, in a boundless plain, in the middle of a wood, in Saxony, without encountering a single companion for five hours, gave me some sensations I had never before experienced. Experience is raining down, but I don't have time to gather up the cheerful raindrops that promise a happy future.

Have a good look at Jean.[112] If you still think he'd be of use to me, tell him to get ready to leave. If I reach headquarters tomorrow or the day after, and see that this war looks as if it's going to last another three or four months, I'll tell him to come. Farewell, *mine libe*.[113] As you can see, I already know a few words of German. Yesterday, in Würzburg, I met two very nice women; they struck me as charming, and took my mind off the sour and ugly thoughts that had occupied me all day long. A thousand compliments.

I think, my dear, that we're heading for Brunswick; it's supposed to be a fine city, with a French theatre. Here, as you might expect, there's a German one; the famous Iffland[114] performs here; I've seen him several times; he seems to act very naturally in the sentimental kind of play, and to have a great deal of naivety in the comic genre – in other words, when he's playing a comic role and has something ridiculous to say, he doesn't show that he finds it ridiculous, he says it out straight, just as fools say foolish things in ordinary life; I gather that he has written some tragedies.

The day before yesterday it was cold and damp; we went to attend a review at Charlottenburg at nine a.m.; I was chilled to the bone; yesterday evening I realised I'd caught a cold and was all out of sorts; this evening I felt the same symptoms; so, instead of going upstairs to dinner, I'm writing to you.

I'm afraid it may be the little fever I suffered from two years ago. I want to stop it in its tracks; it put me in a horrible depression every evening; true, at that time the only thing I had to cheer myself up was my intellectual faculties; I was in Paris, without fire, without light, without any decent clothes, with holes in my boots; here things are quite different. I must have about three or four hundred *louis*; my clothes are all right, but not quite up to the mark; my accommodation is poor and my food good.

On the other hand, my mind is unable to make me either merry or sad; the poor devil is obliged to get some sleep. We're in a little palace where there are four columns supporting a balcony. […]

I'm opposite the arsenal, a superb building next to the King's palace. We are separated from it by a branch of the Spree, whose waters are the colour of green oil. Berlin is situated on a sandy road that starts just before you get to Leipzig.

In all the uncobbled spots, you sink into the sand up to your ankles; the sand makes the area round the city something of a desert – it produces nothing but trees and scrubby grass.

I don't know who came up with the idea of planting a city in the middle of this sand; this city has a hundred and fifty-nine thousand habitants, so they say.

This morning I learned the latest about the army, in whose quarters I am currently lodged, in the *Moniteur*[115] of 20th and 21st.

Here, countless rumours destroy each other every moment; you can only really count on what you actually see.

The sole battleground I've seen was at Naumburg.[116] I'm only the temporary commissary for war. I've written a letter to my grandfather in a letter to you; so please ask him to do what I've asked.

Schoenebeck, 9th November 1806

I'm writing to you from a dismal village called Schoenebeck, near Magdeburg, and on the road from Berlin to Brunswick. We dined on a six-egg omelette that Martial and I cooked, and a soup made out of a few crumbs of bread, some beer and some eggs. Yesterday we visited Potsdam, the apartment of the great Frederick, his tomb. In *Sans-Souci* we saw documents handwritten by him and a volume of his poetry with Voltaire's manuscript corrections. The man showing us all that was one of the hussards of his chamber who was relieved of his duty with the King two hours before the latter died. He showed us a clock given to Frederick by his beloved sister, which he himself used to wind up. It stopped at two twenty-one – the very moment he died.

Send Jean to me quickly. I expect him to leave for Strasbourg on 15th November at the latest. Do everything you possibly can to avoid any delay. We are leaving around 10th December for Warsaw.

Farewell, I am forever thinking of you and I love you with all my heart.

HENRI

Magdeburg has just surrendered.

Brunswick, 25th December 1806

I'm leaving today, Christmas Day, at five o'clock in the morning, for Paris. I'm writing this so you'll know that should write to me quickly: 55, rue de Lille, Paris.

I was due to leave a week ago, but the government and the quarter-master wanted to wait for more material for my mission.

All the preparations for my journey are finally done. The weather is dreadful: a mixture of rain, hail and snow; it's as dark as the inside of a stove; the wind keeps blowing out the candles of the coach's lanterns. Yesterday, at seven in the evening, I'd stopped thinking about this journey; it will have its pains and its pleasures: the chance to see people so dear to me! But to have to leave them a week later!

I'll write as soon as I've set foot in France, at Mainz. I'm travelling via Kassel, Fulda, Frankfurt. The post is so terribly inefficient that we don't receive any letters directly. Perhaps the same happens to the letters we write. Daru is in good health and on the road from Posen to Warsaw.

Look after yourself and love me, and write to me. Tell our acquaintances, such as Mme Mornay, that I'm seizing the opportunity of the New Year to assure her that, although I am galloping from Brunswick to Paris, I love her no less than when Colomb and I used to go for a game at her place.

So don't forget, straightaway!

HENRI

Strasbourg, 30th December 1806

At the stroke of nine I was at the top of the lacy spire of Strasbourg, higher than the bells, and in the middle of a storm-force wind. I thought the spire was going to collapse. I am now en route for Paris where I hope I'll finally hear from you, 55, rue de Lille, as usual; I expect to be there in sixty hours and to stay there for twelve days to a fortnight [...]

I look happy on the outside, my dear Pauline; I will be assured of the reality only when you are married and living in the same house as myself.

This is more difficult; our return to France is not getting any closer; M. Daru is in Warsaw. I came via Göttingen, Kassel and Rastadt. Here, while our horses were being changed, I saw quite a big palace in which Roberjot and company stayed;[117] I was with people who, because of my uniform, spoke to me only on official business. I haven't been able to find out anything new about the catastrophe that befell them.

What about Jean? It really is time to say:

'Go and see if they're coming!'

Lower Saxony, 1807

This German language is a croaking of crows; this morning I started to learn it, enough to get by while travelling. That's my official news.

In fact I can tell you, right now, that I am – I think – happy to have so much work to do: my soul still has the bad habit of being in love, and my reason tells me that this is absurd. Apart from you, I can see nothing that deserves to be loved; in any case, my contempt for the human rabble is growing considerably: they still amuse me, as monkeys acting out farces. I am tired of such ridiculousness, as I have to take the trouble not to lose sight of a single one. When I get bored, I ask my stomach to provide me with a few pleasures.

Farewell; I have to turn my attention to a portfolio whose horrible great maw is the gulf in which my nourishment for the whole day is going to be absorbed. The people I converse with are so dry that I take pleasure in letting my imagination roam at will. I can't read Duclos these days, even though he gives me so much pleasure in Paris, where I had tender sentiments; I am suffering from an indigestion of dryness; I'm reading Ancillon.[118] I have twenty pages to write to you, and not a moment's spare time!

Present my respects to those charming girls my cousins; I am afraid they have forgotten their cousin, the wandering knight, but one thing's for sure – he'll never forget them!

HENRI

Brunswick, 30th April 1807

[…] Honour has been fighting against love and the interests of ambition, which has brought me seven or eight times to the pinnacle of unhappy agitation and ardent happiness all this month of April. On 5th March honour led me to quarrel with Martial; on the 5th, reconciled. I had to leave for Thorn, I conquered love with endless difficulty and, since I must confess as much, weeping; I was so agitated at seven in the evening when I was about to decide to leave that I went running through the streets of Brunswick like a madman; I passed in front of the windows of a young girl I fancy, I felt torn apart, and yet honour was the strongest, I went to tell Martial that I wanted to leave, he was unwilling, he was counting on love to hold me back, he said to me all that was needed to make me stay.

I'm staying, I think I'm happy; I don't know why Minette[119] is starting to make me dance to her tune; politics, vanity and pique all order me to forget her. In a celebrated ball I court another woman: amazement, unhappiness, disappointment on Minette's side. That other woman offers an easy victory to my retreat.

I carry out a superb manoeuvre to get back with Minette. (In the distance, while out walking, I see a man of high intelligence, who despises, as one must, the human riffraff, who has fifty years' experience and an income of a hundred thousand fr.; I go up to that man and talk to him so intelligently in his own way for two hours that he eventually invites me to a party taking place at his home the same evening, and where there were no French; what a fine success.) I arrive at his place full of happiness, knowing that Mlles de Griesheim were going to be there, Minette hadn't wanted to go, I just see her sisters and Mlle de Treuensfels her rival. I am granted a meeting with that rival; just as I am going, I am told, 'If you go to such-and-such a house this evening, you'll find Wilhelmine'. I abandon my meeting, I seize a moment when Mlle de Treuensfels has gone to make tea for me, and I scarper. I arrive at the house indicated where I don't find Minette, but instead the two ugliest and driest creatures in Brunswick.

Yesterday I was finally reconciled with Minette. I could fill two or three volumes if I told you all the silly little nonsense, but I don't want to abuse your friendship by boring you. Yesterday Minette *squeezed my hand*, no more; you'll laugh at me, but after the life I've been leading for six years, that's what I have been so agitated about all this month. […]

The only woman I have any feelings for now is Minette, the blond and charming Minette, with her northern soul, of a kind I have never seen in France or Italy […]

It's likely, my dear, that we're going to have peace.[120]

At this great time, what is going to become of me? Will I be staying in Germany with the troops that are probably going to be attached to other units, will I be going back to France? Or indeed will I be employed on the expedition to the Greater Indies?

Those who set off on such long trips are soon forgotten, otherwise I wouldn't mind travelling far. Of all my dead passions, that of seeing new things is the only one that still remains.

I'm comfortable in Brunswick and often bored. I certainly wouldn't be bored if I went off to fight in Turkey. These are all *perhapses*. M. Daru will leave me in a corner. To seem obedient, I'll have to stay there. […]

LECOEUR, S[ub]-L[ieutenant]

Brunswick, 26th July 1807

My ears are pricked at every minute to know whether or not I can hear cannons firing; my hat and my sword are on my table, my two horses are pawing at the cobbles in the courtyard and growing restive, all because of the Prince de Neuchâtel, Minister of War, who is due to arrive this evening; the whole General Staff is going to meet him this evening at seven o'clock; at nine, there's a play; a big gathering at the Governor's, with fireworks; everybody is running round, everybody is busy. I'm reading Goldoni while I wait: I have come across a fine copy here, which somebody has lent me, six volumes in-8⁰; in each volume there are four or fives comedies, none of them are structured like Molière's, but almost all of them are natural. They have yet another charm for me: they remind me of the manners and language of my dear Italy, the homeland of sensibility. Have you read *Corinne*?[121] Everyone here is delighted with it; but the representation is so very different from the original!

On 11th July, the Emperor appointed me deputy commissary for war; please ask my grandfather to thank whoever was responsible.

M. Daru has a son who is now one month old.

His Majesty has just sent him the cross of the commander of the order of Saint-Henry (order of Saxony), telling him that he was looking forward to giving him new marks of his satisfaction by advancing him in the Legion of Honour.

Martial has been appointed officer in that Legion. He expects to be setting off straightaway for Paris with all his staff.

I do not know what fortune will make of me; these cold spells in Germany are starting to get at me; I'd like to be employed 10 leagues away from Paris or a thousand leagues away. If I were a thousand leagues away, this would give me the right of eventually ending up in Paris itself.

Farewell; I want to tell my Grandpapa about a superb trip to the Brocken (the centre of the Hercynian Forest;[122] it was 25 leagues away from here that Varus was destroyed;[123] you can clearly make out his camp), but having to write 30 letters a day and arrange convoys of every kind means that I have no time.

At least write and tell me why you don't write. Has your confessor told you not to? Is it some kind of a bet? Without my fixed income, I wouldn't be able to eat; make sure you mention this truth frequently.

At the castle of Salzdhasum,[124] *2nd September [1807], 4 a.m.*

You can't imagine, my dear Pauline, the pleasure your letter has just given me; I'd almost forgotten what your handwriting looked like; I opened it as if it were a letter from someone of no importance to me; never has this been less the case! Write to me, please – at length! There is no reason at all for you to throw the letters you write me onto the fire. Don't you know how much I love you? Do I have to say it again?

But write in particular about the charming V.[125] I think you're right; she is a soul of rare quality. I loved her deeply – and I've seen her precisely seven times in my life. All my other passions have been merely a reflection of that one. I loved Mélanie[126] because she reminded me of V. in character. You can guess how precious to me are the least details on V. Does she love her brother[127] as much as you say? He's one of the driest characters I know – just right for the fine society of the present day and age. But I mustn't complain about the illusion that makes brothers worth loving. I simply wish this illusion would lead their sisters to write to them more often.

This sweet thought of V. which, in my soul, precedes more or less all the sorrows which are now present to my mind, came to me in the midst of some superb forests, still fresh with the morning dew, just as, in the company of eight good friends whom I can never for a moment forget to treat with affability, just as we were setting off to hunt for deer. My superior, M.,[128] has fallen prey to a passion for hunting, which means that he views with indulgence – or pretends not to notice – the times when I slip out on Dutch leave from my cave.

I'll be thinking of both of you all day. Try to find out if she has a lover in Paris or Rennes; I almost feel like saying to you, like Our Lord: wherever you are gathered together, I will be among you. What a sweet pleasure it would be, if the thousand stupid vain things separating us allowed us, while we are still young, to spend a day in these dense woods, amidst their vast silence. We might almost find that in the Grande-Chartreuse, but we'd have to put up with social niceties, the Grand-Rue gossip, etc., etc… So, seek your happiness in an embroidered collar, and shun the Grand-Rue.

Farewell, I'm counting on 10 letters from you in 15 days.

By the way, yesterday I killed a partridge. It's the first I've ever killed, but it didn't give me even a thousandth part of the pleasure that I got from a thrush that I killed on the path up to Doyatière,[129] on a tall ash tree, on the right as you go up.[130]

6th October 1807

Herewith, my dear Pauline, are the main works of Mozart, a musician born for his art, but a soul of the North, more fitted to depict the unhappiness and the tranquillity produced by his absence than the ecstasy and grace which the temperate climate of the South grants to its inhabitants. As a man with ideas and sensibility, he is infinitely preferable, the artists say, to all those mediocre Italian authors; however, in general he is quite different from Cimarosa; that's the composer

I'd like to send you; try to read *Il Matrimonio segreto*; *Il Principe di Tarenta.*[131]

Music consoles me for many things: a little tune from Cimarosa that I hum in falsetto makes up for two hours of paperwork. Nowadays, almost every evening, I play piquet with my supervisor, a nice chap who was well acquainted with Collé, Crébillon fils, Rulhière, Coislin, and Letemps, who will be your master in the art of living for a long time.[132] As far as Collé is concerned, the second and third volumes of his journal have just been published; read them: they are very graceful.[133]

What effect did my letter have on my father? Tell him that our consignments of barley are arriving in Brunswick in three or four days; I'll send them to Paris at the earliest opportunity and from there they will go to amaze the banks of the Isère.

Are you still seeing Victorine?[134] [...]

Get this into head: two years of married life, in your household, with one or two children, will change you so much that you won't recognise yourself. I feel it in myself; I now admire many things that I despised 15 months ago. Please, open your heart to Victorine; she is capable of keeping a secret and she has much more experience than you. [...]

25th November 1807

I haven't had a moment free since the second of this month, my dear Pauline; otherwise, I would have told you all about a hunting party after which I stayed in Brunswick for the day. I asked the Intendant and the Supervisor[135] for permission to go hunting for five days in the Harz, a range of mountains 12 leagues away from here. I went with M. Réol, a sensible man lacking in basic education who has picked up a very big dose of common sense from five or six trips to Africa, four to America, two in the seas of the North, and the wars in the Vendée and Lyon. Just we were setting off, or rather, a short while after setting off, we made our coach change direction and took the road to Hamburg. Don't mention this unwise trip to anybody – nobody here has any inkling of it. We arrived in Hamburg after wandering for 45 hours across a vast desert of sand known as the Lüneberg Heath – a really Flemish landscape; vast fields surrounded by wooden fences and cut across by dark pine forests and small streams overflowing to form lakes. At two in the morning we were at Harburg;[136] we hammered away at the door of the best inn situated on the port. We spent an hour shivering outside the door before it opened; a dreadfully ugly servant woman told us, 'Everything's full' and slammed the door shut. We hammered again; the door reopened. We dashed into the house; it took us a whole hour, but we finally managed to sleep on the straw at the back of a barn that had such a snug roof that, as we lay there, we could observe the comet, superbly visible, in the midst of a clear sky (the frost could have split a stone). We were the first to get up, at five o'clock; we found a whole family of Germans drinking coffee in the *stouve*,[137] a room with a stove. It had not been aired since the cold season began; there was something purely animal about the life of those people, with their mournful expressions; their gloom seems so marked that we think they must have suffered some bereavement.

We left our coach with the innkeeper and went to the boat. It was cold and foggy; the boat was crammed with every sort of face – in particular that of a German fop, his pipe, and his valet: a frigid caricature, whose vulgarity of thoughts and feelings soon inspires one with indifference mixed with contempt. At least a French fop is pleasant; he feels self-esteem only if he can amuse other people. Of the foreign fops, the most acceptable are the young men who find a way of satisfying, cheerfully and prudently, the tastes of their age; by 'prudently' I mean that they offend nobody, since the tastes of young people often involve neglecting danger. Harburg (pronounce 'Harbourg' in French, all *u*'s in German are pronounced 'ou', unless they have two dots over them, *ü*) is located on a lock that leads to one of the mouths of the Elbe. At Harburg, the Elbe is huge: during this season, it covers several small islands and on the 28th October, the day we passed by, it was over half a league wide at Harburg. Réol is an experienced sailor who's been shipwrecked two or there times; he explained all this to me in the language of sailors, which has at least five or six hundred words that are French only in their grammatical form. [...] The sailors went so slowly that we were almost on the point of capsizing; these little dangers, which I had never experienced before, gave me considerable pleasure.

Réol told me that while he was sailing in North American waters, a great gust of wind blew the ship almost horizontal; it remained in that awkward position for a few seconds. A second gust of wind righted it.

We stopped off at Altona and finally entered the port of Hamburg, full of ships slowly rotting away because of the absence of trade.[138]

(I'll take a break here; all morning I've been taking things to stave off this annoying fever I get every winter, and I can't go on. Mme Daru[139] is leaving tomorrow for Paris.)

Now it's the 27th and I'll carry on; but I prefer to continue with the parenthesis than with the letter. Mme Daru left yesterday; today, we've got real northern weather: it's not yet four o'clock and I can barely see through the two big windows that look out over a square. I have thought of you twenty times over, today and yesterday, while reading novels whose only merit is that they are written in English. What a false picture of society these novels give; you'd say they'd been written by, and for, the inhabitants of the moon.

I'm afraid you may have formed several of your opinions on the basis of **these damned books**. Only beautiful souls have these sorts of illusions; but such souls are almost all unhappy, and I tremble in case you increase the number of them. You'll see from Bigillion's letter (attached) that several old gossips of the Grand-Rue have spotted your attempts at disguise.[140] If you don't take care, you'll never be married; I don't think I'm exaggerating just for the sake of it; I give you my word of honour that I consider marriage, in general, to be as useful for the happiness of women as it is harmful to men. I'd give anything at all for you to deserve the friendship of Mlle Victorine. Do anything at all to ensure this, and let me know the result. She has experienced the cruelty of the world towards unhappy people – that false pity worse than contempt.

What makes follies so fateful for the beautiful souls lodged in women's bodies is that these follies are always attributed to some contemptible weakness, generally speaking. The wittiest and most loving man would not marry you if twenty or thirty women assured him they had seen you running round the streets at night dressed in a man's clothes.

Two years ago, when people gave me advice of the kind I'd like to see you following, I said to myself, 'A cold soul!' and made sure I didn't believe a word of their advice; but many bad things that happened (I didn't tell you about them because they happened every day and would take too long to go into) finally opened my eyes. I made up my mind to take a good look round, to assure myself of the facts that were related to me, and to base my opinion only on the ones that were positive. I'd give a year of my life to see you in this same frame of mind.

'But I'm just so bored! I can't go on leading such a monotonous life!'

But remember that once you've got involved in some scandal, it lasts forever; no more husband for you. We'll have an income of maybe four to five thousand francs; you'd lead a life very similar to that which D… has with a revenue of ten thousand; she has public opinion on her side; she has social circles in which she is received with pleasure; if anybody raises objections against her, these are drawn from her person, her wit, her character. Now you are a thousand times superior to her in all of those aspects, but your very superiority will damage you.

'But I'll teach English, drawing, etc.'

You imagine that such a job will give you enough to live on and that you'll be as happy with the four thousand francs that you earn this way as the *bourgeois*, your neighbour, is with the four thousand francs that he earns from his trade in *filoselle* stockings. Not at all: the stockings seller will look down on you and will find a thousand ways of making you feel his contempt. If you'd seen anything of the world, you'd know that any person whose social status is not high enough for vanity to have to esteem, together with a certain fortune, is the object of the most cutting contempt – it may seem outwardly polite, but it is really hurtful. Try and imagine that from those **damned books** I mentioned just now; you might as well try to work out what a windmill looks like on the basis of a plough. The truth is just the opposite of what they say: it's as simple as that. If they showed the world as it is, they'd fill people with horror and – even on the people who share their opinion – produce an impression of gloom that their readers would shun.

So a man of wit and commonsense, writing a novel from which he hopes to make some money and a build up a reputation that will help him sell the second one more easily, takes great care not to tackle this fateful question. He depicts passions as did the Abbé Prévost, and he depicts them as they are found in wealthy people. And yet poor Abbé Prévost didn't have very far to go to find examples of wretchedness: he had run away from his monastery at twenty-five, and from that age to sixty-seven, I think, when he died, he had to put up with the most disgusting things.[141] If, instead of running away and causing a scandal, he had used his intelligence to obtain his secularisation by intrigue, he would have been a well-considered man of letters in Paris, a member of the Academy, the lector of some prince, and with an income of thirty-five francs, like Duclos.

I'm citing this example as it's the shortest to explain, and you may already know the characters in the story; but the world is full of facts that produce the same result.

A woman needs to be married, first and foremost; it's what people ask of her; after that, she can do what she wants. I keep coming back to the example of Mlle Victorine. They say she's leading a retired life near Grenoble; try to go and see her with Mlle M… and there, pour out your heart to her (but don't mention me at all): ask her for advice. She has a beautiful soul; your frankness, and the unhappiness you are about to fling yourself into, will touch her; she will give you advice that might not be same as I give you, but will certainly be more valuable.

I wanted to send you from Hamburg some small pictures to give you an idea of the area: but I could only find views of Dresden, the Florence of Germany. Here they are. Put them up in your bedroom; they're all quite different; every time that you see them, reflect on that danger of incurring the wrath of society, especially when you have soul and wit; you can pick yourself up with a certain amount of low cunning, but it's not possible otherwise. I'm including with my letter a map of Germany and part of Europe; it's a really convenient map, as you can always have it in front of you. I'd already marked my travels **through the world** on it: as I can't get hold of another copy, I'll send you the one I've been using.

One remark struck me today: three quarters of *bourgeois* risk their fortune or at least lay themselves open to ridicule in order to do something that will make them seem superior – travelling post-haste, for instance, or other things of the sort. We find them hilarious; but the tiny shred of authority that we all exercise gives us the chance to enjoy, for nothing, the same pleasures of vanity as those for which the *bourgeois* paid so much money. In the past few days we've had five or six anecdotes which lead to this conclusion. Perhaps it will seem unintelligible to you. But I have to go to a reception at the chief judge's – there will be eighty people there.

Tell me how they have been employing Jean. And send me one or two moulds of our ancestors' seal. At the same time, send my regards to Mlle Victorine. Farewell; love me, and write to me. I wish the bitterness between my father and myself could end; try to reconcile us. What do people say and think about me? As you can see, you really must write to me – you are my ambassador.

Durand

3rd December 1807

I spent the whole of yesterday evening directing a play. It was great fun, and I'm still basking in the enjoyment I derived from these dramatic forays: we rehearsed *Dupuys et Desronais* and *La Vérité dans le Vin*,[142] a vivid, realistic picture of the manners of that age; Marianne, though not exactly pretty, wasn't bad. A pretty women who comes into a gathering of men adds a brilliant varnish to all their qualities. Yesterday I had three witty men among my actors; we laughed until midnight.

I have spent the whole morning with Gregory VII and the whole Middle Ages. I'm reading Koch, the same book I recommended to you.[143] I'm going to combine it with Ancillon and the *Essai sur les moeurs* by Voltaire; and then Condorcet's essay on *Le Progrès des lumières*.[144] I hope, with the help of these men who are driven by different passions and prejudices, to draw up for myself a broad panorama of modern history. I don't know why the Middle Ages are associated, in my heart, with the idea of Germany. The peasants of the Brunswick area have preserved *exactly* the dress of the age of Charlemagne. The North, which makes me bad-tempered in spring and autumn, touches me in wintertime: it appears decked in all its sombre splendour. A gothic church, surrounded by decrepit churches and covered in snow, touches me. I've got one just like that next to the place where I'm staying: Saint Giles.[145] I don't know if you'll understand all these associations of feelings – perhaps you feel the same way, since I've discovered that in many things you and I are alike – but, this morning, I was absorbed in Hildebrand[146] and in the courtyard of the castle of Canossa, with Emperor Frederick, I believe.

You may find some remarks in all these ideas: there are very few people with whom I dare to share them; but it may add a certain weight to the advice I'm giving you and that you might otherwise think comes from a frigid soul. If you mention this detail to my friends, they'll be able to tell you to what exorbitant degree I took my prejudice against what I called the 'frigid'; just three years ago, it all went as far as despising Duclos.

The only thing I can count as authentic experience is that which misfortune has engraved in my heart since 16th October 1806.[147]

Can you believe it? Two-thirds of my ideas have changed since that time, not about principles, but the way one should behave in company. When you have the misfortune not to resemble the majority of humans, you need to regard them as people whom you have mortally insulted, and who put up with you only because they are unaware of the way you have insulted them; a word, some trivial gesture, can betray you. So stay patient until your marriage: once you are married, everything takes on another colouring; with a bit of attention, and the art of getting your husband to believe that he's more intelligent than you, you'll be able to do pretty much as you please and you'll finally be happy in your own way.

B[runswick], 24th March 1808

I can retire from my honourable post as preacher, my dear Pauline, since I see you and Mlle V.[148] have now got together. She can give you much wiser advice, much better adapted to the circumstances. But beware of annoying the vulgar crowd by appearing to be *too* intimate with her. There's another bad habit against which I am forever preaching: you always start writing your letters to me at 11.30, so that all your letters are cut short by the post leaving. Just let it go, and write me some of those lovely eight-page letters that it is so enjoyable to receive from the people one loves, especially when you happen to be exiled in some devilish hole of a place.

I know it inside out. So nothing interests me. I've just been galloping across the fields for a whole hour. I didn't see a single new thing. Same goes for my morale. I've been invited into the noblest social circles in town: 10 gaming tables, one for faro, and a *schneiden* (I think this means 'to cut' or 'to trim'); 7 or 8 little girls to whom I regularly make 3 or 4 insipid remarks made ridiculous by exaggeration or *mannerism*, otherwise they wouldn't understand them. In any case, you feel these people are always on the alert with you. This makes it impossible to be natural, and thus to enjoy yourself. But it's 1 o'clock; the post really is about to go; so this letter is just a rapid part-payment. Tell me in detail about the way the Mall[ein] ladies[149] are treating you. Love me as I love you, I mean boundlessly.

26th March 1808

I can well imagine, my dearest, that you must have a thousand things to do, a thousand duties to perform; you'll hardly have time to read my letter, but I enjoy writing to you; I'll enjoy reading and rereading your reply even more, if you have time to write one. It seems to me that, in sensitive souls, there is a host of melodies that, as it were, float around; all of a sudden we are affected by the feelings they express, they come back to our mind and we hum them for days on end, always finding new pleasure in them. That theory is the story of myself, today; a charming melody came to me, on the little words *cara sorella*.[150] In my memory I relived all the time we spent together: how I didn't like you when we were children; how, once at Claix, I gave you a beating in the kitchen. I took refuge in the little cabinet of books; my father came back a moment later, furious, and said to me: 'Naughty boy! I could eat you up!' Then there were all the bad times inflicted on us by poor Aunty Séraphie;[151] our walks along those paths surrounded by stagnant water, towards Saint-Joseph. How I would gaze at the mountains sloping down towards Voreppe, and sigh! Especially at twilight, in summer, the slopes were outlined by a mild orange colour! How intensely I thought of that name: *Porte de France*![152] How much I loved that word, *France*, for its own sake, without thinking of what it expressed! Alas! That delightful happiness that I imagined for myself – I glimpsed it once at Frascati, on a few other occasions in Milan. Since then, there's been no sight of it, I am surprised I ever felt it. The mere memory of it is stronger than all the present happiness I can procure for myself.

Such are my daydreams, my dearest; I'm almost ashamed of them; but anyway, you're the only person in the world to whom I dare tell them. I've realised something rather sad; when we lose a passion, we gradually lose the memory of the pleasures it gave us. I've told you that at Frascati, at a fine firework display, just as they were going off, Adèle[153] leaned for a moment against my shoulder; I cannot tell you how happy I was. For two years, when I was overwhelmed by sorrow, this image cheered me and made me forget all my misfortunes. I had long since forgotten it; I wanted to think of it again today. I can see Adèle as she is, in spite of myself; but, as I am, there is no longer the least happiness in that memory. Mme Pietra Grua is different: her memory is linked to that of the Italian language; as soon as, in a woman's role, there is something that I like in a work of literature, I involuntarily place the words in her mouth. […]

I can't get used to not receiving letters from you. I am well aware that when anyone gets married they bankrupt half the friendship they extend to their friends; but I want my half, and you're giving me nothing.[154] Since the misfortune that befell us, I've had no news from Grenoble.[155] It's a foreign city to me and although I don't like to stay there, it's still the place where a dozen people who are constantly in my thoughts live.

So give me some details, and never fear that you might be giving too many; above all, tell me about your wedding; I almost hope that everything will be over by the time you receive these lines; tell me all. In order to encourage you to relate trifles, I'll be the first.

A few days ago I found myself one thousand three hundred feet under ground: at the bottom of a mine in the Harz called 'Dorothy'. It's strange; but, as is my bad habit, the spectacle that most amused me was the sight of myself. I have such an aversion for nasty smells that they overcome me all of a sudden; I was afraid of that odour of carbonised sulphur that you smell in foundries. This was the first thing I hated the idea of; the second was falling. You go down vertical ladders [...]; if your hand slips, you turn into mine slag; those greasy rungs are so laden with slimy mud that your hand is forever slipping.

It had the same effect on me, in miniature, as if I'd been fighting on horseback in a marsh. From the distance, it seems like an undignified position to be in; when you're there, you're busy successively surmounting many little difficulties; the first little successes you meet with give you boundless joy and eventually seem entertaining, since they give you a reason for feeling self-esteem, and you're happy to have reasons for such an unreasonable thing.

After that, the King[156] arrived; I was presented to him; I went everywhere and was greatly diverted by my companions. I've struck up a friendship with one of the lords in his court, a man who turns out to be well worth being liked. Women, Italy, music, war, ambition are all present the same way in our hearts; our minds are less alike. If we ever had to act together, we'd soon be complete friends; up until now we have been agreeable acquaintances to one another.

Four years ago, I was in Paris with a single pair of boots with holes in them, without a fire even though it was the middle of winter, and often even without a candle. Here I am a personage: I receive several letters in which the Germans call me *Monseigneur*; the great French personages call me *Monsieur l'Intendant*; the generals who arrive come to pay me a visit; I am in demand, I write letters, get cross with my secretaries, attend ceremonial dinners, go out riding and read Shakespeare; but I was happier in Paris. If it were possible to move one's life to where one wanted, like a piece on a draught-board, I'd still be going to learn the art of declaiming at Dugazon's,[157] going to see Mélanie with whom I was in love, with a shabby frock coat, which really tore my soul in half. When she wasn't prepared to receive me, I went to read in a library, and finally, in the evening, I'd go for a walk in the Tuileries where, from time to time, I envied those who were happy. But how many moments of delight in that unhappy life! I was in a desert where, from time to time, I found a spring of water; I'm at a table covered with dishes, but I don't have the least appetite.

This monotony may perhaps change: they think that we are going to punish Austria for all its insolences; but personally, I'm not one of those 'they'. I have no wish for war and would stop it a thousand times over if I could; but once the business has been decided, I'll be delighted to see war waged and be part of it. It's at this point that we can almost always say 'You never see again what you've already seen', and I'm starting to realise that it is on this condition alone that three quarters of men and things are tolerable.

Farewell; write to me; go into the same little details; make sure that the enclosed ground at Claix is planted out as an English garden. That's the nice side of the land where I'm vegetating; every corner is transformed into an English garden in spite of the water, the sun, the air and the soil, and sometimes I find a moment of life in these pleasant imitations of a nature from which I am too far away.

Dubois

Well, my friend, what do you have to say about it? Was it worth getting so scared about?[158] I will admit, however, that the moment when M. Stupi sang the epithalamium must have been somewhat scabrous, especially for a woman. But if that day occasioned you some embarrassment, it gave me a very intense pleasure in the charming description that our excellent grandfather gave of it; there is one of my life's main tasks safely in port… And there you are, already off on your travels; don't spend your money on jewels and other foolish things, save it to go and see Milan or Paris; but before you do, fix a sum of two to three thousand francs that you mustn't exceed.

I quiver with happiness like a child at the thought of the address I'm going to have to put on my letter.

I'll recommend one thing to you: an English garden. Choose one of your properties and plant it this winter. – 'But what if I don't plant it right?' Never mind! Acacias, chestnuts, poplars cost four francs to plant and give more pleasure than walls which cost ten francs per current measure. One league away from Vizille my brother-in-law has a very picturesque piece of land; it's near Claix, it would be charming; choose a place where nature has done a great deal, and plant it during the first year of your marriage; in fifteen years you'll be able to stroll under those trees with your children. […]

H.

[1808] [about May]
[The beginning of the letter is missing.]

… little house that appeared to be on fire in the plain below us. To get there more quickly, my noble neighbour left a road and dashed towards a high elevation that I thought was cut off.

All of a sudden, I lost sight of him. I reached point A, and I thought I was going to take a tumble, and at point B I was going to encounter ---an 80-foot cliff; unless I bring my horse to a halt at A, I thought, I'll never be able to rein it in at point B.

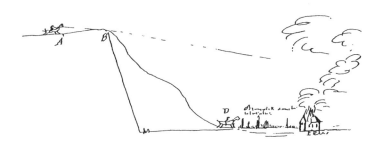

Brunswick in the distance. – Fire.

But, through a narrow escarpment in the terrain, I'd just glimpsed the little chap D galloping towards *Fire*. My weakness filled me with shame. Let's do our duty and leave it in the lap of the gods. On reaching point (B), I found a way down, quick without being (too) dangerous. I spurred on my horse v. hard – he was an excellent mount, in fact, and reached the fire in a moment. The fire was soon under control. If I'd been a bit more of a coward, I'd have arrived in time to see my riding companion being blessed by those good people, who'd initially thought they were doomed. I'd thought the terrain sloped like B-M; if it had been, I'd have done the same as young Curius.[159]

After this splendid image, I'm going to give you a great proof of my trust in you. But I'm assuming that you'll give me your word of honour that you'll burn the attached cipher. Put it to good use, but burn it as you do all my letters. I demand a reply; just a word or two: *I have burnt everything.* You can copy an extract from it before burning it, but you must destroy it. Here is the reason: I love you more than my brother-in-law, but I don't want to fall out with that fine young chap. I'm counting on a word from you within 24 hours.

Have my corner bedroom in Claix made up.

[Signature illegible]
Captain

I thought I was rid forever of all the pomps of love, and on the point of saving my soul, but my pride has just been thoroughly humbled: I've just received a letter that gave me so much pleasure that I am forced to conclude I'm in love with the woman who wrote it.

So here's my tale: eight months ago, there was a colonel with whom, by virtue of my rank, I struck up an acquaintance; he had a twenty-three-year-old wife, a woman of considerable intelligence, with that elevated character that I so much like in Italian women.[160] I joked three or four times with her, once in particular when I won a couple of *louis* for her at a game where you stake six *sous*. Her husband went off with his regiment, but he died six leagues from here. She came back a few days later; I went to see her. I find that she receives my visit, in the midst of her deep grief, quite properly, but just like she does everyone else. So there I am, received like everyone else, feeling bored, knowing that she's feeling bored too, sure that I can always spend some agreeable times with her – I let four long months go by without going to see her. One evening, while I was out for a stroll, chance brought us together: she was leaving a week later; since that moment, we've been spending our lives together; she knew the same cities in Italy as I did, and almost the same people; she leaves, and I gallop ten leagues to her carriage door. We have the most ridiculous conversation in the world, all night long; she practically doesn't go to bed, since she wants to talk of the pleasures of hunting and other interesting things; but I think that our eyes showed more spirit. Finally, I leave her; on the way back, galloping so hard I break my horses, I feel too stupid for it to be natural. She'd promised she'd write to me; bah! she forgot all about me. The day before yesterday, a scrappy little letter was brought in to me, on yellow paper; so very elegant that I thought it must be from Barral. I open it and, a good quarter of an hour later, I find that I'm blushing to the ears, striding up and down in agitation, the happiest of men, uttering a lover's sighs.

Isn't it comic to think that it was quite in my power, for four long Brunswick months, to see or to have a charming woman, and yet I waited until a mere three hundred leagues separated us before I would think of it?

On top of which, the day before yesterday, i.e. the 10th, a battle! A fusillade at which I was present, where an old woman, both hands crossed over her stomach, had the privilege of having them pierced like Our Saviour, and her stomach too, whereupon she departed forthwith to experience the effects of his mercy. Not to mention several sabre thrusts which nobody is keen to boast of. The moon was shining in all its magnificence; the broad street was crowded. The cry of *Fer-flou-Ke-ta-Françau-ze*[161], which means f… French rascals, falling on me from every side at the sight of my army hat; a rifle shot; twenty people stretched out all round me; the others rushed to huddle against the walls, I was the only one still standing. A pretty young woman of eighteen, her head almost under my boots… I think she must have been wounded; she was shivering violently, but not because of my hand, which was quite innocently feeling a very pretty and tender arm; I piously lift her up to see if it's her leg which is broken; battle is joined, new rifle shots ring out; I carry her up against a wall; I was thinking of Sganarelle carrying Clélie[162]; I put her down; she stares at me, makes a pretty little bow and takes to her heels.

Meanwhile the soldiers are dashing up… Here, my style becomes more humble as the hero vanishes. He found himself in the midst of a people rising up against the French, one of whom had happened to kill a civvy; he was attacking the hospital where the killer was lying, and one hundred and fifty brave soldiers were opening fire on the aforesaid scumbag. I can remember this event because of the superb coloration of the scene: the light was as pure as the eyes of Mlle de Bé…[163] – but that's a comparison à la Chateaubriand, who depicts the countryside of Rome as if it were Babylon. Mlle de Bé… is a grown-up young woman of seventeen who has as many attractive features as her ancestors had titles. She has big eyes, dark blue, set off by the most beautiful white in the world; eyes that, through their radiance and purity, pierce you to the depths of your soul; there's something immaterial about those eyes; a soul lies bare.

Well, write back to me. **Has our great father write to mister D[aru]?**

M. Duboin
Captain

[19th April 1809]

My dearest,

I'd been intending to write you a long letter, then a diary containing everything I see and the countless little things I feel and that you would have felt too. None of it has happened. I don't have a minute to myself. I haven't had a wink of sleep since the 12th when I left Strasbourg, except in the coach.

This life fills me with delight. I'm in my element. ¾ of the things don't seem worth getting involved in. Here, the things that need to be done demand such a rapid response that I'm almost always on the alert. These last two days, I've travelled 20 leagues every morning before breakfast.

I think that tomorrow or the day after the Austrians will be beaten near Ingolstadt[164] – we are leaving for there in 2 hours. I have to run – out in the street they say our horses and our coach are being stolen.

So write, soon.

Burghausen, 29th April 1809

The day before yesterday, the 27th, we left Landshut[165] to come and arrange lodgings for M. D[aru] and our seventeen comrades in Neumarkt. The road was filled with two rows of munitions wagons, and since there were occasions when only one carriage at a time could file through, we stopped every now and again and had time to examine the countryside, which is charming. It is covered with woods of pine and fir. These woods are generally square in shape, and the way in which they are placed on the hills surrounding the road makes them resemble from afar infantry regiments that have come to a halt. We were permitted to entertain military thoughts. There'd been fighting two days previously on the terrain we were crossing. I could examine the bizarre disorder that war produces. The most striking thing is the quantity of excellent fresh straw, still standing upright, sown in the fields. Every half hour we would come across a bivouac. But apart from those little straw huts, the fields were strewn with them. You could see caps, shoes, many shabby cloth jackets, wheels, the shafts of carts, many little square pieces of paper that had been wrapped round packets of cartridges.

From time to time, a tall hill allowed us to see one league or three quarters of a league along the road, we could make out in the midst of the choking clouds of dust two ranks of cuirassiers threading their way between the convoys, sometimes at walking pace, most often at a trot, and leaping into the adjacent fields as often as they could. In the middle of the road, an artillery convoy, at its sides hundreds of carriages bearing the baggage of the regiments, and the carriages of the officers who, every league or so, found some excuse for getting out, swearing and attesting to heaven that they'd fling the whole lot into a dungeon. It was by these polite means that, having left Landshut at two o'clock we reached Neumarkt, which is only six leagues away, at around ten in the evening.

You can imagine that the bacchanal was even more hellish in a small country town of two thousand souls who suddenly find they have a population of forty thousand men who haven't had dinner and don't give a damn about anyone or anything. We scurried around from ten o'clock to two in the morning arranging lodgings. Then I busied myself using a little twopenny knife to cut some slices of beef from a thigh that I'd managed to get from somebody in Landshut. Sleep fell upon me in the middle of this operation. I slumped down to the foot of the table; a big black dog had the impertinence to come and lie down on my feet. I left him there, for the sake of peace and quiet. One hour later, a deserter, a soldier who was Austrian but had been born in France, whom I'd taken on the day before as a servant, came to wake me, bringing my slices of beef – they were more or less cooked, but were covered with a crystallization of salt. I was just tearing into them with my eyes closed, when I noticed through a chink in the shutters that day was starting to dawn. I opened them wide, and saw G[ener]al P. with a braided hat, sitting astride a bundle of hay tied to the back of a cart.

'So, General, where are you off to like that?'

'To my brigade. They say there's going to be a battle today, and I'm in despair. I don't know how I'm going to get there.'

'Since you're in despair, come and share a piece of this beef from hell.'

In he comes and gobbles it down like a thief. He found the beef nicely done. Whereupon there arrives a courier for M. D[aru]. A quarter of an hour later it's M. D[aru] himself, who tells me:

'My word, you'd better go and arrange lodgings at Alt-oeting,[166] maybe your dashed impertinence will succeed again.'

So we left at half past four. On the road there was an even bigger chaos than the day before since this terrain had been the site of a battle more recently. However, the dead had been taken away, as they had the day before.

On arriving at Alt-oeting, we found the Imperial Guard. Two generals and fifty grenadiers around the poor devil of a municipal officer in charge of lodgings, who couldn't understand a word of the intolerable gibberish being shouted into his ears; he answered, when we spoke to him in German:

'Monsieur, I no parlez-vous French.'

The generals had forbidden anyone else to be lodged with them, and I took refuge in the claims a boss has to get the best lodging in town. Everyone was uttering menaces, swearing, yelling, in that horrible little room. Finally the stench drove the combatants away. I trudged to my lodgings through a downpour of rain. I found a little countryside farm surrounded by bivouacs. I dried myself by a fine fire that some grenadiers had lit, and returned to try my luck in that stable of Augeas. I'd turned a huge inn upside down to make a lodging for M. D[aru]. I bumped into my comrade who had arranged the lodgings for all our general staff, I purloined a billeting order from him and finally reached a no. 36. Here I found a countess surrounded by six children; the eldest, a daughter of seventeen, wasn't very pretty, but fresh of complexion and above all with a nice figure, and she as well as her mother could speak French. The small children had superb eyes. I put on an air of mildness, and deployed my finest German phrases, by means of which I was, within half an hour, the object of their adoration, and ensconced in my superb room, though it had neither fire nor bed, and leafing through *Moore's Voyage in Germany*.[167] Here I sought for some ideas different from those I had inevitably been obliged to think over the past twenty-six hours, when the mother and her six children came into my room.

'Monsieur, the Austrians, they are here! One of my farmers has just now come in and told me, and I thought it my duty to warn you.'

'Madame, does your town have any moats?'

'Not at all, Monsieur; in any case, my house lies outside the city. If you'll come up with me, you'll see the Austrians.'

During this colloquy, which was longer than I have made out, Mlle Rosine showed a great deal of interest in the fate that awaited me.

'The battalion on the square is going to be driven back and you'll be taken prisoner, there's no doubt about it.'

I was much more preoccupied by this friendly face appearing to me in the midst of all my dark ideas than by the approach of the fearsome *Kaiserlich*,[168] but we eventually climbed up into a tower whose windows had no balcony, and only with the greatest difficulty did I prevent the little children from throwing themselves out of the window, and even I went too close. Mlle Rosine held me by the arm; finally we looked up and in the gaps in the woods surrounding us, we did indeed see the heads of five or six cavalry regiments with grey coats. But I recognised them as cuirassiers from our side – they'd taken their white coats because of the rain, that had turned them grey, and we all came down, laughing at this great danger, though my thoughts were all of Mlle Rosine. I forget everything until seven when M. D[aru] arrived. There were many people lodging with my countess, I made a speech or two telling them not to make any palaver, they responded with some mockery, but in the end there was no noise. When I left, Rosine did not come with me, but her mother came and made me promise that I'd spend the night at hers so as to prevent any noise. I promised. I went off to have supper with M. D[aru], who, at around eleven, said to me:

'It wouldn't be a bad idea if you left straightaway to go and ask the Prince, who's at Burghausen, etc., etc.'

I'd got some requisitioned horses, but they'd just that minute escaped. My deserter had gone to bed, nobody knew where; while I was at the Countess's, sixty men of the Imperial Guard and all the men employed by the army station had turned my house upside down. To crown it all, it was eleven o'clock, pouring with rain, not a cat in the streets (which were quite unfamiliar to me), the only light came from the distant bivouacs around which you could make out shadowy figures passing back and forth. The comic aspect of my situation stopped me losing patience. Note that, as I'd been praising Rosine to my comrades, they'd immediately proved to me that at no. 37, next to my no. 36, there was a much prettier young lady. This was the final straw. M. C[uny], who I'm travelling with, assured me that I was a sybarite, that it was up to me to go and look for horses, in this town where I didn't know anyone, where everyone mistrusted us, where nobody would open his door even if he heard it being broken down. He urged me in particular not to forget that we would be leaving in one hour.

So I started to threaten everything and everyone, even the big black clouds that were drenching me in the most dreadful downpours. I told my story at every door, saying that I had a mission of the highest importance. My importance didn't persuade anyone. They kept replying: '*Kein pferd*. No horses!' Finally I had an idea, and added a few details to my mission. I said that if I didn't take to Burghausen the orders with which I had been entrusted, all the troops there would go short of bread the next day. This bright idea worked. A score of soldiers had been unable to get billeting orders and had decided to settle down in the very same off[ice] where these orders were issued; they now started to argue among themselves. I heard them, and requested that they open the door to me. One of them came to unbarricade the door. Once I was inside, and sheltered from the rain, I became twice as eloquent and eventually, an hour later, I presented myself at no. 36, with four huge horses, and three peasants to lead them, all soaked to the skin and even worse.

I found M. C[uny] laughing with Mlle Rosine and her mother. He'd gone and remembered that he'd left behind some wretched sabre – not even sharp – at Neumarkt, and had sent a courier to fetch that valuable weapon. So he told me he'd wait until two o'clock for his courier to come back. During our absence a second colonel had come, and taken the Countess's very own bed. As for me, I'd given the lodging I had in her home to M. Joinville, my old friend from the Army of Italy.

We started to dance, to sing and tell stories, and every now and again I went to take a glass of brandwin[169] to our peasants.

Mlle Rosine was having a very good time, she showered me with her attentions, but she also seemed to be getting on very well with M. C[uny]. The spell was broken. Finally, a great deal of laughter, the bells chimed half past two, the sabre still hadn't turned up. The good German who had been carrying the despatch didn't suspect that there was an answer and had met halfway another courier coming from Neumarkt to Alt-oeting, and exchanged his despatch with his comrade's. The Countess wanted to serve us some more coffee, she'd put an egg yolk into the cream; so we finally set off, feeling very satisfied, at around three.

Our horses were a little restive, but C[uny] and I fell into a deep sleep. We awoke this morning at around five, our horses galloping down a steep slope. We cried out like eagles, brought them to a halt, and had them shod.

The Salza, a river that runs more swiftly and is a little broader than the Isère, is here sunk into a bed of sandstone, its banks are some three hundred feet high, and so shifting that just a few trees, that are starting to have some pretty little leaves, can grow on them. Just where Burghausen is, the Salza has eroded the western bank, and a small plain has formed there on which the town is built; but it is devilishly steep, which is what woke us up, and on the other side a very steep slope upwards.

We can do no more than look at it. I'm writing to you from a monastery where I'm staying. The bridge over the Salza is right nearby. But the Austrians have had the good sense to burn it down. There are nine arches, the river is very rapid and from time to time I interrupt my letter to go and see this picturesque labour. The whole army is having to wait here because of this bridge. Here Bavaria comes to an end, the other side is Austria. Yesterday M. D[aru] was laying a bet that we'll be in Vienna by the 13th.

This morning, on arriving, we took our despatch to the prince. His reply was a demand that one of us should set off and gallop hell for leather to Alt-oeting. It was raining even more heavily. I in turn proved to M. C[uny] that he was the one who should go and leave me to arrange lodgings.

I've never sworn so much in all my life. My throat is sore as a result. I finally discovered my monastery where, a quarter of an hour after my arrival, I was presented with a very nicely done eggnog, with two slices of lovely white bread. This eggnog gave me a good laugh. But I can't carry on, the bells are chiming six o'clock, I'm waiting for the boss and he's still not here. M. C[uny] has gone off to bed, I'm dropping with sleep, I wanted to give you a brief sketch of a day on which I thought of you more than twenty times. Everything that moves me makes me feel these sentiments afresh. Today, Mlle Rosine is forgotten. I'm standing in front of a bad copy of a lovely Madonna by Guido.[170] I spend my life gazing at it, trying to work out what was in the painter's mind, and then going to see the bridge and the swift-flowing Salza which every so often sweeps away to the devil the fine pieces of wood which they are trying to cross it on. Farewell; best wishes to everyone, especially to those who don't care either way. A couple of days ago I saw M. Duplan who never stopped talking about M. Gagnon, Mlle Zénaïde, etc.

Vienna, 15th June 1809

Still don't have a moment to write. Working night and day. Riding, women, and divine music the rest of the time. Unfortunately this 'rest' is all too short. In spite of all the reasons for not writing, I must write to congratulate you on your non-pregnancy. Get out and about, gallop away, see Milan, Genoa or Berne. You'll be tied down all too soon. I've never been able to understand the mania for having children, pretty little dolls who turn into fools who make you want to run away, unless they get a good, independent education, and who has the patience to provide them with such an education?

Vienna has one of the loveliest climates I've ever seen. There's just not enough time to enjoy it. In the middle of it all, the heart is lonely. Last night I consoled myself **with the Deserted Village of Gray**.[171] […]

I've just written a long letter to my father in which I describe my political position at length.

I'm still suffering from the fever I mentioned, but it doesn't have much influence on the situation of my soul. I'm happy, though agitated by the passion I mentioned. I don't pay much attention to anything else; we've been in Vienna for over two months, and this period has been as nothing to me. Recently I was sent on a mission to Hungary;[172] I promised myself as I left Vienna that for a full twenty-four hours I wouldn't think of what was within that city. This was perhaps the one opportunity I would ever have to see the celebrated land of Hungary. I discovered a superb country, magnificent vines, a narrow, superb road embellished with a row of young chestnut trees on either side, the road stood out all white amid the verdure of the meadows and the harvest, the view changed every half hour; on the left, to begin with, the imposing Schneeberg (or snow-mountain), and then, as the road carried on from that white summit, the countryside becomes both mild and majestic; instead of small mountain peaks, there are long ranges of hills stretching out and, on the horizon, a big lake named [***] On leaving Vienna, I went to Laxenburg,[173] where there are those wonderful gardens and the amazing 15th-century castle. You yourself would shudder at the sight of those poor chained Templars who painfully look up when they see strangers descending into their tomb.[174]

From Laxenburg I went to Eisenstadt and from there to the shores of the lake that you can find on the maps. Here I found the Croatian costume in all its purity: it's exactly that of our hussars, with moustache, little boots with a silver edge, etc., etc.

I've told you, I think, that before returning to France I was supposed to be going to Warsaw and Naples. I'll need to. Leaving Vienna will break my heart; but a fortnight later I'll have only agreeable memories of it, especially while travelling.

Haydn passed away here, about a month ago; he was the son of an ordinary peasant, who rose to immortal creation thanks to the sensibility of his soul and the studies that gave him the means to transmit to others the sensations that he felt. A week after his death, all the musicians in the city gathered at Schotten-Kirchen[175] to perform Mozart's *Requiem* in his honour. I was there – in uniform – in the second row; the first was filled with the great man's family: three or four poor little women in black, with mean, pinched faces. The *Requiem* struck me as too noisy and didn't interest me; but I'm starting to understand *Don Giovanni* which is sung in German, almost every week, at the Widen theatre.

I don't know if you received the musical score I sent you from Brunswick, I think it was. At the end, Don Giovanni sings an aria under the windows of someone or other,[176] accompanied just by the violin,[177] it's the aria that follows that one that makes the greatest impression on me:[178] we always gallop there as fast as we can to hear it; yesterday, we came just as it was ending; we couldn't be bothered to dismount and went to see the ballet *Paul et Virginie*.[179]

Farewell; my letter is pretty rambling; but even as I write to you, I have something else on my mind. Give me news of Victorine's soul. I still love the woman I thought she was five years ago. Farewell, write to me often.

PS – My grandfather mentions the B[eyle] girl cousins, but in obscure terms. Tell me what's happening. Are they thinking of increasing our fortune? In that case, I could abandon my uniform a few years early. By the way, I was forgetting why I was writing to you: couldn't you come to Italy at the same time I'm travelling round that lovely land? Make the most of your spinsterhood-marriage. Once you start having children, you'll be a slave. What a pleasure it would be to see Italy with you!

Vienna, 6th August 1809

The object of my passion is almost completely lost without my having derived the least bit of pleasure from it all; today my life is that of the cruellest of tyrants, gnawed at by the blackest and most humiliating jealousy, without having had a moment to draw breath. This was one of the loveliest days in the year; my friends spent it in what may be the most delightful place in the world, Schönau, six hours away from Vienna; an English garden that's so natural that you never think of art. Their day, which they have just been telling me about, has all been a matter of sweet and pastoral sensations, so to speak; mine has been quite dark, atrociously dark. I'm sure that the person I love most and whom I would be proudest to please is deceiving me and has been led to deceive me by the contempt and boredom that I have inspired her with. You are a sensitive soul; these few words will explain my rage. However much I gazed at the charming English garden behind the Auersperg Palace,[180] nature did nothing for me. It was like a man whose mouth was full of nitric acid being offered a glass of sugared water. The thing that touched me the most was a swallow flying between those charming trees; I envied its fate, free from passion. Anyway, this evening, worn out by pain and unable to feel anything else as my feelings had been too strong, I took refuge in the *Matrimonio segreto*; but it's no good, I know it by heart; still, it took my mind off things for a few minutes.

If we have peace, I'll see Italy, even if it's only a corner of it. – I'll go and see Bialowieska;[181] I need a loved woman to chase away the horrible darkness that accompanies me everywhere.

Vienna, which is a charming city, washes over me; all I can see here is the woman I love and can't have; to add insult to injury, I'm ill. I need peace and quiet to get better, and never was I further from them. However, if I have nothing further to hope for, I'll gain relief in a fortnight by plunging helter-skelter into another passion, but I still have much to suffer until then, especially if I still have moments of hope every now and then.

Farewell; a letter from you is the only calmative I can imagine; it would cool my blood. Give me some news about everything happening in Grenoble, and embrace Périer for me, and dear Lucie.[182]

Vienna, 29th November 1809

Yesterday evening I was sent on a mission that means I can get away from the S[ankt]-Pölten HQ. Just as I was setting off, one of my friends whom I'd asked round to share my dinner, which consisted of a few potatoes and a scrap of tough meat, suggested that I go to Vienna when I came back from my trip.

Why not straightaway?

'But will they let us through without official papers and without passports?'

'We'll see. Let's send out for some post horses first.'

I issue the order, the livery of my coachman has the desired effect, and the horses are given us without any official papers. We set off at half past nine. All along the road we are stopped by our guards, and, half asleep, we reply in German. They chase after us, uttering oaths, and we have some difficulty in getting rid of them. A little further on, already asleep, we're asked in German who we are; we reply in French. We are given some more post horses, but the man in charge orders the postilion to deliver to the Vienna police a note giving our details. We'd been planning to dismount two hundred yards or so from the barrier, to enter on foot, and to send for our carriage via our friends' horses. We stay awake for a couple of hours, then we doze off only to be awoken by the Austrian sergeant at the gate asking us who we are. On leaving we'd left our uniforms off, but with sufficient forethought that my friend had left on his uniform waistcoat, and I my hat. So there was no way we could pretend we were anything other than French officers. We boldly give the names of two of our fellow officers back in Vienna. They make a few objections, but we seem so sure of ourselves that they finally let us through. We wake up three of our friends who are all staying together, and they tell us that the Emperor Francis II is going to St Stephen's to attend a *Te Deum*. He arrived the day before yesterday in a shabby post calash, but with six white horses attached. He was recognised near the city centre, when the *vivats* rang out on every side. They wanted to unharness his horses so that they could pull him to the palace themselves. He urged the horses on, repeating the words, 'I thank you, my children'. No sooner had he arrived in the Burg than he re-emerged on horseback and for two hours showed himself to his people, who, it appears, were filled with enthusiasm.

When we got to our friends' place this morning, we needed to find some round hats. We were told we couldn't wear our uniform hats –

a few Frenchmen were badly treated the day before yesterday, when public enthusiasm was high. But none of the hats fitted my big head, until they finally unearthed an old opera hat, which I pop on, and all five of us, rigged out in the most grotesque kit you can possibly imagine, head to the Burg. The snow was coming down in horrible great gusts. The guards and the people prevented us getting any further. Finally we hear cries of *vivat!* and, after a picket of cavalry and forty or fifty lords or lackeys covered in braid, we make out a small, slender man, with a insignificant, worn face, saluting comically. Francis II wears a three-cornered hat that he puts squarely on his head; to salute he lowers his head directly in front of himself, without bringing his hand up to his hat, like someone saying *yes* from afar.

We go to St Stephen's, a magnificent gothic church, not renovated like Reims cathedral, but left in its venerable dark grey like the one in Strasbourg. In the midst of the crowd, I heard five or six times: '*Das ist auch ein Françose*. That's another Frenchman.' This was usually said in tones of curiosity, but two or three times with hatred. We can see from the distance that they're not letting people into the church. I casually ask the two German sentries:

'May we enter, gentlemen?'

'*Oh ya her guade*.'[183]

With the greatest politeness. We make our way into the church, where there were forty or fifty members of the clergy in grand albs, thirty or forty men of the city, and lackeys. Immediately we hear 'It's those Frenchmen again!' on every side. I position myself near the entrance to the choir. A silence in which you could have heard a fly reigned among these people, gathered here to celebrate the presence of an emperor they greatly loved. On every side we kept hearing, '*Françose, Françose*'. As I looked on, with all the men wearing their decorations around me at the entrance to the choir, I spotted Mme Salmi, the most beautiful woman in the city, they say (she has the face of a Raphael Madonna who's hit thirty, but her eyes are expressionless, though in general she has divinely lovely features); she smiles and I say to her, in a loud voice:

'I am fortunate to see, on the last day of my stay in Vienna, the most beautiful woman and the most remarkable event'.

Everybody turns round and I see a smile on every face. Francis II, looking even more seedy, insignificant, worn out, tired, a man who needs to be wrapped in cotton wool so he'll have strength enough to breathe. He was closely surrounded by four tall officers of the crown, drenched to the bones as he was. Since I had this at least in common with them, without however being obliged to listen to the *Te Deum*, the first bars of which suggested it was going to be a fine piece, I came back to get warm, I found nobody home and I am writing in the heat of the moment to tell you my story while the *Te Deum* is still being sung and they are firing off discharges of musketry under my windows. […]

Dubois
S[ub]-L[ieutenan]t in the 7th

Paris, 19th February [1810]

I'm happy, my dear friend; if I had a letter from you, I'd be very happy. My appointment as A[uditeur][184] seems certain. Tell my father that I've just been assured that the A[uditeurs] would be placed in order of the presentation of their cases. So I await confirmation with impatience.

This change in status that makes me so happy as far as ambition goes doesn't allow me to remain near what comprises my real happiness. I don't have any regrets about the life I've been leading for four years. If I'd been an auditeur then, I'd be a prefect by now, but then I wouldn't have seen Berlin, Brunswick and Vienna; Wilhelmine, Charlotte, and Babet[185] would be unknown names to me. That's a lot of names, but what does it matter whether we gather happiness from some feeble annual plant or from an eternal oak? I'd be sure of my harvest if I could be sure I'd be seeing you this year. Try to come and spend two months in Paris. I have so many things to tell you!

I was tenderly moved yesterday evening, you'll make the acquaintance of Ottilie.[186]

Foulques

13th April [1810]

I'm sending you, my dear little lazybones, via M. Dalban, a vol[ume] of Chamfort. Since you don't come to see me, you might send me some money to buy books with.

I'm convinced that Baron Cabanis must have bored you.[187] Were you struck by the theory of the 4 temperaments? Try to observe it in nature.

Chamfort does not have the same principles as Helvétius; as a result, he has a black vision of things. He thinks that man loves evil for evil's sake. He had a scurfy humour[188] which always put him in a bad mood.

The best things in him are the extracts from Duclos and Richelieu. I am contented.

I don't think I'll be in Burgundy for at least a month. They're putting on the *Matrimonio secretto*, and some wonderful concerts. The only thing that would complete my happiness would be to have you here.

Put on a dinner for [***] and [***], often. If those two characters were a little more sanguine, they'd be very nice men. But two bottles of *Hermitage* make everyone feel sanguine for a few hours.

I'm glad to see you've left your apartment. I've left my jealousy behind, too, but young Jenny is avoiding any private meetings and is scared of me. It'll never end. It's a passion that I've grown on an espalier to produce the greatest number of sensations possible. If I'd actually had her, there'd have been far fewer sensations.

The Président de BROSSES[189]

Best regards to your husband. Push **the father for the title**.[190]

28th April 1810

Do you know, my dear Paula:[191]

The curfew tolls the knell of parting day,
The lowing herd winds slowly o'er the lea,
The plowman homewards plods his weary way,
And leaves the world to darkness and to me.

I was deprived of this imparalelled piece since my departure of Wien,[192] and, this morning, in this beautifull weather of spring, I came at Raynouard's and found an exemplary on great letters, perfectly convenient to my view. If you have never read Gray's works, you shall thank me for the hint. The fairest thing I could imagine in french, should be the elegy of Gray translated by André Chénier. If you ever make verses by amusement, undertake this little work. This elegy has not 200 verses; you can copy it in a borrowed exemplar. How are you with the design of seeing Paris this year? I have been glad of the progress of His M. till Anvers;[193] that gives

me a fort night delay. This journey is the dearest of my wish. If you come, I will tell you the sentimental pleasant story of the next to it. Nothing new for my affair. It is proper that our grand father should write to M. Z.[194] I fear I have a little neglected to write to this grand father. Make my excuse for that, if necessary, and remember, every day morning, that perhaps it is the last allowed to us.

> On some fond breast the parting soul relies,
> Some pious drops the closing eye requires;
> E'en from the tomb the voice of Nature cries,
> E'en in our ashes live their wonted fires.

Gray came two times at Grande-Chartreuse and even wrote a little sensible[195] ode in father's album. If I can reach his complete works in four volumes, I will accurately search what he wrote to M. West; his intimate friend, of this awfull scene. When you come there, read the elegy in a seal which perhaps provided the author, with many a sensible thought.

Paris, May 1810

We arrived at the Sèvres factory at about 11.[196] Just now, it's surrounded by trees with fresh foliage; I'd say that it's situated in the midst of quite a pleasantly variegated countryside, if I didn't think there were too many houses in the neighbourhood. But as far as the Paris neighbourhood goes – and its distinctive character, in our view, is that it is quite lacking in grandeur – it's still very nicely situated. Here we saw the most handsome living creature I've ever set eyes on, Adolphe Brongniart, the son of the scientist who is the administrator of the factory; we also saw the most handsome manufactured object I have ever seen, the round table that is one inch short of being three feet in diameter, with the portraits of most of the marshals[197] and of the Emperor, in the middle. Isabey,[198] who had the physiognomy of a thespian stringing along forced expressions of politeness before a powerful man whom he fears and does not like, without the least trace of grandeur (***celestial fire***), did us the honour of showing his table, which really gives one the idea of perfection, especially in the portraits of Marshals Soult and Ponte-Corvo; Princes Davout and Berthier are the least handsome. This charming work of art needs to be fired one day, and this may break it. The rest is quite good; a stained glass window that transmits the daylight through the pretty figure of a sitting woman. I suggested to M. Brongniart that he create some nocturnal designs for the windows of a boudoir; he agreed with me, but told me that experiments in that genre hadn't so far been a success.

The sculpture is only middling; they ought to ask Canova and Thorwaldsen for models; in general, these ones don't capture the grandeur of the Emperor's face, which they reproduce endlessly. We saw an emperor, one they'd put on horseback, with a vulgar, pretty-pretty face.

On our way out, we met M. de Marescalchi with the whole of Italy. M. Z.[199] wanted to show them round his factory; we left them and set off for Versailles. The road was pretty, fresh greenery everywhere, we soon reached M. de Cédat's place in the Cour du Dragon. The streets of Versailles are those of a capital, and its shops those of a provincial town. The apartment and the society of M. de Clédat likewise, especially a certain M. Daguesseau, a little Escarbagnas[200] in quality, and his wife, a tall, chubby-cheeked woman, with a blonde wig, whom he calls Pauline.

We left for Trianon after a glass of excellent Malaga; M. Clédat, although a little bit fixated on Versailles, is not without wit, and proves as much by having some excellent wines, but without ice; a real shame.

The Trianons are very pretty; nothing melancholy, nothing majestic about them; the furnishings[201] are not fine enough for a sovereign who wishes to play that role; they sometimes (especially the beds) lack comfort. Every time we came across something worth seeing we ran into M. de Marescalchi and his troupe. We were merry, amused, running hither and thither. Pretty furniture in mahogany, a pretty painting of the Battle of Arcole, poor busts of the family with tasteful inscriptions, just the names, Louis, Joseph, Elisa, Pauline; the Emperor's bedroom, small, not very comfortable or tranquil, all on the level, with four fine etchings,

The Maid of the Garden, *Belisarius*, *The Upbringing of Achilles*, *The Rape of Deianeira*, I think. Very pretty English garden in the Trianon: there are tall trees, which is the great merit of English gardens, and valuable trees, which is a kingly pleasure and means nothing to me; but it's a great deal for souls who cannot rise to the love of the beautiful.

I forever have in tow Mme Elliott, a pleasant woman, although really not very pretty, and thirty-one years old. I was astonished, a week ago, to find no affectation and no timidity in a provincial woman; but that's because she isn't one: she was brought up in Paris; I had found pleasure in Sèvres and it has not abandoned me since, coming ever closer to me minute by minute until ten in the evening when I left Mme Nardot's.

I don't know, my dear friend, whether you'll be able to decipher this descriptive fragment and whether it will give you any pleasure. I spoke to the g[ener]al about the trip to Lyon, and in his view it should be postponed, but if this makes things too difficult, to go for it. Don't breathe a word. **Do you make a** diary? It's a way of laying up laughter for later years. I've just finished a volume started in Marseille, four years ago. I was really young at the start. I realised that, at that time, I hadn't sufficiently borne in mind the fifteenth octave of the XVIth canto of *Gerusalemme*[202] which I suggest you reread.

Let's enjoy this day and not count on the morrow. That's what Horace said in Latin 1900 years ago, and it's what we need to do today, or give up any idea **to the happiness which I shall find with you**.

Sorbon
L[ieutenan]t

5th May [1810], 2 a.m. [Paris]

I've reread your letter 20 times, my dearest. Yes, it's her.[203] I thought that things might work out one day; but we mustn't break up. I'm very far from being wealthy enough to get married. I couldn't stand the idea of living in Paris without my wife living in the same social circles as myself, and, for that, you need 20 thou pounds' income at least. So I have to resign myself to a bachelor existence. This has become perfectly clear to me as I've thought it over for an hour or so. But these weren't the reasons I turned down, a month ago, a really fine match that my lady protector wanted to arrange for me.

What? She's going to get married? When, and who to? **I did think that her brother** had made her think poorly of me. At least, he gave me to understand, in a bit of a quarrel we had a year ago, *that after what had happened* we couldn't be friends as we had been. However, I may have behaved like a man in love, or not very sensibly, the two things are very similar, but I was always very gentlemanly. Please try and find out what Mlle V. thinks on this score. I would feel grievously wounded to learn that she thinks I've behaved badly. But, let me repeat, you mustn't do anything to prevent it all from happening. I would be mad to think of marrying.

You have to agree that she's a woman of character, and far removed from the insignificant dolls who garnish the salons. As soon as you can, tell me the name of the man in question, and let me know. Is she going to stay in Grenoble? You can guess how precious her least little word is to me. You know that even the way words are arranged in a sentence depicts the feeling that has dictated it. So report her words about me, exactly as she said them, or will say them, to you. I talked about her (but without being too explicit) a great deal, and about you too, my dearest, with M. Lejeune, whom I saw briefly. He must have left today for Rennes. It's a part of the world I was about to go to for her sake, but anyway, it's too late to even think about it now. I've burned your letter and I expect one from you in a week, reporting word for word what she said about Henri.[204] Mallein wrote to me a year ago, saying that she was making fun of him, which rather pained me, but I thought that a couple of words spoken with frankness and honesty would make her come back. Farewell, it's time to end and let things end.

1810 [Paris]
[The beginning of the letter is missing.]

… constancy in the objects one studies: this is one of the secrets of happiness.

Here, at random, are the titles of books that I have enjoyed, rightly or wrongly.

Letters of Mlle Lespinasse,[205] the truest depiction of 18th-century love in Paris.

* *Seven Years' War* by Archenholz, 1 vol. in-12^0. One finds oneself taking a tender interest in Frederick II.

Tasso, Dante, Alfieri.

* English tragedies by Mlle Baillie.[206]

Tom-Jones, in English.

* *Lifes of poets* by Johnson. *His preface to Shakespeare.*

* *Letters* of Bolingbroke *on the study of history*.

* Williams, *Governments of the North*; a really serious study. Rhulière mentions the author in his *History of Poland*. He was highly critical of his way of life; that's what made me buy the book, and I was right to do so – it's excellent.

Duclos's novels.

Works of Chamfort, 2 vol. in-8^0, which I advise you to buy – excellent.[207]

* *Memoirs* of Beaumarchais.

* And, all the time, Shakespeare, for whom my passion does not grow, simply because it cannot grow any more.

I can send you *everything that is* starred. At least confirm that you've received my letter. Did you get my little Gray?

Reassure our good old Grandpapa about my business – it's going just fine. Success is probable, but not certain. I'm not leaving for Lyon for 8 to 10 days. If H. M.[208] goes to Italy, don't fail to see that great man in Lyon or Chambéry. Yesterday I ascended the column in the Place Vendôme.[209] It's the only perfectly beautiful thing I've seen completed here. I contemplated the statue of the Emperor, I was clinging to one of his thighs, 160 feet above the ground. Superb view. Talk money **to our father**. I absolutely need to borrow 6,000 fr.; but a *loan*; I don't want any gifts. I have got used **to the matrimony of thy friend**.[210] A thousand fond regards to P[érier].[211] Have you had my letter franked and sent off to Lambert?

Have you read *Corinne*?[212] It's excellent when it's not horrible – overblown and full of fake sentiment. There are great truths in it. Mme de Staël aims to compose a work: 'The Spirit of the laws in

18th-century society'. As soon as she starts tackling this subject, she's excellent, and mediocre when she strays away from it. What she says about the total absence of vanity in Italy is absolutely true. I observe it all the time in the Italians who are here; and how far it is from Paris to Rome!

DUFOUR

Monday, 2nd July 1810

Our little family celebration was charming; the couplets composed by Picard who, with his livery on, played with us, were charming. The first effect was a sense of tender affection; then a great deal of laughter. Two hundred people arrived; Fitzjames made us laugh; after which there was dancing; I was the last to leave, at daybreak. I'm telling you this as if it had taken place a thousand years ago. Yesterday was Saint Martial's day,[213] we had a thoroughly family dinner at M[artial]'s place; at half past eight, Mme Z. set off tranquilly for a party that was being given by the Prince of Schwarzenberg, Ambassador of Austria.[214] Since his residence would have been much too cramped to receive a thousand guests, they had – as at all the parties given recently – constructed a huge room made of pinewood. The floor of this room was raised three feet above the ground. To take away the smell of pine as the weather was so very hot, they'd painted the inside of the room with turpentine, so I've heard. Just as the party was going full swing, and as His Majesty was doing the rounds in this room, a candle fell and set fire to a curtain. People assumed it was nothing, but once the curtain was alight it set fire to the wall of the planks of wood against which it was placed and, at one and the same time, *like in the time it takes to perform an exercise*, is how M. Z. put it when he told me of this accident, the whole room was ablaze, the sides and the roofing together; the fire in the ceiling burned through the cords of the chandeliers which fell onto people's heads; the floor caved in at several points. You can imagine the cries, the tumult, the horror, then the position of those who had escaped this pyre but could not find their wives, their husbands, their children. The poor Princess of Schwarzenberg, the Ambassador's sister, fell victim to her maternal love.

What makes this accident unique is the terrible contrast between extreme gaiety and the most horrible event one can conceive of, especially the dreadful claps of thunder and a horrible tempest. Fortunately our excellent relatives were not hurt. [...]

7th August 1810

Things couldn't be better, my dearest. A man it's impossible to get hold of has given me an extremely favourable audience. You'll say I'm like all men of ambition, but being [***] isn't enough; there are 300 a day of these; you have to distinguish yourself. The whole advantage comes from the fact that, on 1st August, I had to distinguish myself from among 6,000 young men. The number of councillors is reduced to 300.

How did I win this victory? By making the conquest of M. Z.[215] How did I do that? By making sure that people everywhere say nice things about me to him, and doing him honour in every sense of the word. For 4 years I've behaved in a logical way, I spent money on nothing else. I haven't acted, not even for a quarter of an hour, ever since a certain Monday when, in the morning, in his room, he refused point-blank to make me what I now am – I haven't acted for ¼ hour without thinking of the goal I wished to reach. I've had some initial success. The g[eneral] whose aide-de-camp I am has given me bonuses. I used them to please him even more. Unfortunately, I've used up all my savings, and just now, **my father sends me four hundred livers.**[216] **So unequal a sum is but** a drop of water in the middle of a drought. So try and get him to understand, from the proper point of view, my current situation. 2/3 of the path are behind me; I hope that half the remaining third will be behind me after 12th August; but anyway, however prepared people may be to give me a position like that of M. Camille P[érier],[217] but I still need a year or two to serve an apprenticeship and, during those years, either I will inevitably snuff it, or I'll need an income of 7 to 8,000 francs per year, if I'm a mere a[uditeur]; if I'm at Court, 16 or 18; but in that case I'll have a salary of 6,000 fr., and my position will enable me to borrow a few little things here. Repeat these arguments to him in twenty different guises. I'm right. In this way the means to convince him will rain down on you. **Speack to self-love and vanity. Make our uncle an auxiliary power**. Above all, repeat, repeat, repeat. **I understand very well that my conduct appears very singular, eyed from the province, but speack and let our father speack with the reasonable Alphonso,**[218] **he has seen the true and will testify it.** In a word, be an advocate, a talkative, obstinate advocate. They're the ones who succeed. You see, I've succeeded after a siege of four years – but it needed a continual siege. Make sure lack of water doesn't lead me to perish at the moment of triumph. **Our father in the same very wondrous letter by wich he gives me twenty-five *louis*, says to me that he has here sex thousand livers**. Make sure that he will **lend me that money on interest, but think upon a thing: I will not a pound from thy husband.** This relationship of creditor **to debtor** would kill our friendship, and it's too precious for me to expose it to that danger. **So we must have all from the father**. Burn this and reply.

Make sure **that Alph. speack to our father of the spency**[219] **of the great town**.

Meudon, 19th September 1810

I'm just back from Paris where I left Faure[220] setting out for Grenoble. I've entrusted him with the task of finding 6 to 8,000 fr., whatever it may cost, if **our father** continues to refuse to help me at this decisive moment **of my life**. Félix **is a man perfectly raisonnable but a little bashful**. He'll go and see you. Give him a warm welcome, indeed a warmer one than you would for anyone else, so he'll feel at his ease. I'll be in your debt. He's quite incapable of abusing any welcome he is given by turning into a bore and visiting too frequently. You can open your heart to him on everything regarding me. He knows a great deal about my current activities, and will give you some accurate information about the character of a certain person. F[élix] has been kind enough to say he'll bring me back a few books. Give him all the help you can in the diplomatic mission he's agreed to carry out on my behalf.

We're having a lovely month of September here. I've tried to make the most of it, going twice in succession to Champagne. I was recalled twice on business, and I'm stuck in Paris. I went out into the country-side with a very witty man and we found that the only thing missing in our happiness was that we had nothing to love. Chateaubriand[221] would say: just a little of that feeling gives a voice to nature. Without love, nature is soulless and dead, and inspires us with nothing more than a frigid admiration. You may perhaps have read in my little volume of Chamfort that the worst *mésalliance* is that of the heart, and this friend and I are both suffering from such a *mésalliance*. We are tied up with women who don't understand the best part of us and whose esteem for us is based on trifles; for example, the woman I am seeing esteems me for my air of hauteur in social life. Our real principles on the topic of the hunt for happiness[222] sound in their ears like sonorous phrases that we utter just to be witty. The greatest happiness that could befall me would be for you to spend a few months in Paris straightaway, and, in a few years' time, spend every winter with me in the capital. But if we desire the end, we should also desire the means. You're a woman of sense and, at the same time, you have the art of bringing others round to wanting what you desire. Use these two great qualities to increase the fortune **of my brother** and especially to quieten his anxieties on this head. The other Péri[ers] are all unhappy. You can apply the title of a novel by Surr[223] to them: 'Splendor and Misery'. Two of them here have 30 thousand *écus*; the Prefect[224] has 64 thousand fr., the least rich has 18,000 fr. income, and I would not advise any of my 1,800 fr. clerks to swap his happiness for theirs. Since I really like Alphonse, analyse this unhappiness. It seems to me that it comes from the *need to be led*. They would be excellent soldiers in the war of life, but they are bad generals. Alph. has a decided liking for you, I think, thanks to the instinct that tells him you would have led him to happiness by persuading him that the path down which he is advancing is the best possible one for him, and that he should distinguish himself on it. That's the only flattery permitted and its effect is irresistible. That's what makes Mme de N. so adorable. On leaving her place, everyone is more contented with the position that chance has allotted him. And this opinion has a real effect; it gives them strength and gives them the ability to seize a happiness that was previously out of reach. Tell me what you think about this idea of living together. Even if I do get married, I'll still love you more than I will my wife. As I write, I've just been ordered to go straightaway to Paris to go and carry out an inspection at Versailles. I don't know what exactly.

DU BOIS

Give me some news of this distinguished soul Miss V. M. and of his matrimony.[225] It strikes me she could be found someone better than a **fox with 8,000 fr. Her brother** would find a nobody with 10,000 fr. I know at least 5 or 6 nobodies, all with 10 to 15 thousand, who wouldn't resist the flowery prospect that this marriage would open up to them and a nobody is worth more **that a bad fox**.

10th December [1810]

I bet that, after all my letters about the b(aronetcy), you think I've become a nasty ambitious fellow with hollow, wrinkled cheeks, an envious eye, etc…[226] Not at all. I'm more chubby-cheeked than ever, and the day before yesterday I came out with something worthy of a sensitive young man; I'll tell you about it to raise myself in your estimation. So, I was having dinner at the home of M. le comte Jaubert. I found, sitting next to me, M. Amédée P. He's one of my colleagues. So I there and then yielded to the pleasures of old acquaintanceship, and we talked about Gr(enoble) throughout the dinner. I found the dinner went on a bit, since I had three evening engagements: 2 of pleasure and one of duty. When M. A. had talked a lot about G(renoble), he told me how he had come back from there, saying that he had travelled slowly, because he had been with his mother **and the miss** [***] who had even praised to the skies Thuélin[227] and the mistress of the household. **At the name of this once so beloved girl, all my sentimens were awackened.** So I managed to learn **from him that this very evening** he was going with **this miss to a box** that he'd hired at the Variétés, to see *La Chatte merveilleuse*[228]– everyone in Paris is running to see it. I myself hurried as fast as I could to get rid of my travelling clothes and get to the theatre as fast as my horse could carry me, for here I hoped to see her. I arrive: *no more tickets*, except in the 4th floor circle (roughly speaking, 6th floor boxes where the lackeys' seats are). I climb up the stairs and, with the help of a lorgnette, discover **the brother** at the back of a box, at the front of which there were 6 women. I can't make her out distinctly. Now and again, thanks to a graceful gesture, I thought she was a woman in a short black jacket; a minute later, I thought a blue hat must be her. I completely strained my eyesight. I manage to punch my way out of this elevated pit and rush down to the first floor by seducing three of the usherettes guarding the box entrances in succession. In the first circle, I was offered a seat less than twenty yards away from her. I didn't dare take it. I hope this was the timidity of real feeling. She hasn't seen me for 4 years, and I don't think she's ever seen me wearing full mourning; my reason kept telling me all this, but since it isn't reason which guides love, I refused the seat in the first circle. It was the only one. I was obliged to go back up to the second level, from where I stared through my lorgnette until I was half blind, gazing through the frame of the box. Impossible; I just couldn't make her out. But I only left when she came out. I trotted sadly off to one of my evening engagements and was obliged to tell repeated lies by way of apology to the two others. All my running round at the theatre was particularly meritorious in that it was horribly packed and all the usherettes, ticket inspectors, etc.… were twice as strict as usual. For the big rat and the two mice of Cinderella, transformed into a coachman and 2 grey little lackeys, are filling the whole of Paris with ecstasy – and it really is a charming piece of nonsense. That's what I think about my evening, too. And yet I do want to see her.

If my current way of life continues and you don't come to Paris, I think my heart will grow completely ossified. I'm like that bachelor that everyone kept encouraging to marry; I don't fall in love, or hardly ever, and nobody is in love with me. And in this society, if you have any experience at all, you are only ridiculous when you express a feeling which you cannot defend yourself against. You adopt the habit of seeming hard-hearted so as to escape looking ridiculously prone to affection. […]

D'ALRIMPLE

I have just been really happy, my dear Pauline: the holy feast of Christmas Day left me with a little tranquillity; the old inclinations of my soul led me to read, and to pick up a book suitable to the studies that fired me with enthusiasm during the years of poverty that I spent in Paris. So I read with pleasure, putting the book down twenty times over, the first eighty pages of Burke's book *on the Sublime*. I was distracted every few moments by my current ideas of ambition, and then I felt regret at no longer living amidst those noble, intense, and tender tears that were forever preoccupying me when I was living in the rue d'Angivilliers, opposite the fine colonnade of the Louvre, often not having even six francs in my pockets, I would spend entire evenings contemplating shining stars setting behind the pediment of the Louvre. For the past six months I haven't had time to reflect on any of the things I've read, and my reading matter has been restricted to La Fontaine's novels, since you can pick them up and put them down at any minute. While reading my copy of Burke, I kept breaking off to reproach myself for this or that visit that I hadn't paid. Some powerful friends have lent me money; I've got a nice apartment, simple, noble and airy, decorated with some delightful engravings; I tried to enjoy it with the soul I had in 1804; it's no longer really possible. I have a superb view from the window of my little study; I could gaze at the sunset through the rain and the great clouds rent by a storm wind. I longed for Bellisle;[229] he's travelling post-haste to La Rochelle on a mission. He left yesterday and I'm on my own for two or three months. I kept mechanically opening the drawer of my desk where I put the interesting bits of paper.

I opened a little letter: it was from you; never have I sensed with such rapture the pleasure of loving you. This charming letter was dated Wednesday 15th March. But what year? That I don't know. The stamp is on the edge, and all I can read is 20th March 18… Everything you say is in perfect harmony with what I feel. It's exactly another myself that I'm reading. The conformity of the handwriting added to this charming illusion. I feel the pain of being deprived of your letters intensely. I'll send you the charming letter you sent on 20th March. Read it and send it back to me. If you read it, you won't be able to resist the desire to write to me. As for me, I am shedding hot tears as I write to you: so let's talk about other things.

I have in front of me a charming engraving by Porporati,[230] with the title *Il Bagno di Leda*. Idle and curious spectators would resort to their usual exclamation on seeing it: *Indecent!* All the same, I advise you to buy it (it costs fourteen francs); it's a third of the painting by the divine Correggio in the museum; in the engraving there are three women, two swans and an eagle. Next to it I have the portrait of the divine Mozart which I bought in Vienna from Artaria, who knew Mozart well and assured me it's a good likeness. The *Nozze di Figaro* is on tomorrow, but I'll be forced to miss the first half to go to a house where I was introduced last Wednesday; I stayed there for a quarter of an hour and saw Mme Récamier, a charming woman; Mme Tallien, not very charming, but remarkable. If only you were in Paris! Try to come in 1811. However, I'll not conceal the fact that I'll certainly come to give you a hug, even if I have to desert! My desire to see you is too strong! Farewell, you whom I love more than anyone in the world! Tears are rising to my eyes… Burn my letter.

1st February 1811

I've just had a disagreeable experience, especially in view of the idea it inspired me with. Four years ago I made the acquaintance of a likeable young fellow, gentle in manner but quite popular because of his great good sense; he was an auditeur and was appointed to an important post in the provinces. He spent four years there, and came back a week ago; he seemed to all of us as to be a vulgar creature, a boring fool. I was struck by this change; I've often seen this kind of thing, and I've worked out the cause – which is this (as agreed yesterday by all of us): he attached too much importance to the opinions of others, and this was his sole failing in Paris. This failing wasn't dangerous: chance had placed him in an elite society, composed, apart from the rest of us young men, of men known for their intelligence. He went out into the provinces and, little by little, without realising it, was infected by the plague. This malady even helped him to become happy. The provincials shocked and annoyed him to begin with; after the first year he acknowledged there was something in what they said; the second year, he decided that our train of thought and our way of being happy were over-sophisticated; the third year, he thought the people he was administering were only occasionally wrong; finally, the fourth year, he could no longer understand his old friends, and grew angry as soon as anyone dared to question the fine prejudices on which he sleeps with this ear and that. By making perfidious concessions, I managed to draw from him the entire history of the progress of his malady. This seems incurable: people make fun of him, he bitterly defends his peculiar way of looking at things, and once vanity (that great and sometimes sole passion in France) has been set in movement, nothing can stop it.

Alarmed at this example, and thoroughly convinced that, *without a judicious mind, there is no solid happiness*, yesterday evening I got myself a copy of Tracy's *Logic*.[231] I passed on the message to everyone that I had a migraine; I went out for a coffee at nine o'clock, it's now 3 a.m. and I've got to page 176 of this *Logic*; I hope to finish it in a fortnight. It is my intention to re-read it or look through it at least every year, so that my mind will always be open to the light, and that if I ever came across anyone who told me, 'Raphael's virgins are not the most divine figures in the world', or 'The music of Méhul is better than that Cimarosa's', I would be able to listen to his proofs, and accept them if they were correct.

Have a good look at yourself. Might you not have picked up, by chance, a few of the commonplace and false ideas that you must hear being repeated every day, and which you quite rightly pretend to applaud? Might it not be a good idea for you to take the same antidote as myself, who am in a less unhealthy place, and to read the *Logic* of that good fellow the Comte de Tracy? All of this in secret – and laughing it off if anyone finds you reading it. Grace is merely weakness; a woman's graces reside in her shape; she'll cut her own legs off if she allows herself to be caught studying.

Farewell, my dear friend; preserve yourself from contagion and try to reason justly in all things. Even if Molière himself were to appear before me and tell me, 'Mme So-and-So is coquettish,' I'd ask him to give me his proofs. True knowledge, in all fields, from the art of getting a turkey-hen to hatch an egg to that of creating the painting of *Atala* by Girodet, consists in *examining*, with the greatest possible precision, the *circumstances of the facts*. That is the whole of Tracy's *Logic*, to which I would add, 'Never take anyone's word for anything'. […]

18th February [1811]

I'm letting you, my dear Pauline, in on a secret that I haven't mentioned to anyone in the family; so pretend you don't know. I've been told I can expect to be given a mission, one of two that are on offer. **The first for Lubeck, the second for Rome**. You'll guess that I am much keener to get the second. Only one thing bothers me; I can't call by to give you a hug en route; since I am travelling to examine what may be of use to illustrious visitors, I'll be travelling via Lausanne and the Simplon Pass. I'll only have a week to get to Rome. I'll be spending two months **in the fair Italy** and, on my return, I'll tell you all about *le cose vedute*[232] over three or four days. Only one thing annoys me – the lack of money. I'll be reduced to borrowing at nine per cent. It's awful, but should I miss out on a mission that's useful and will allow me to shine? I've written with all possible frankness to my father and my grandfather, saying that there was only one thing I could do – a mortgage loan at five per cent, six thousand francs every year for five years.

Urge the baronetcy and all that.

All these considerations are depressing since they show that my father does not have for me the tenderness or at least the *enlightened* tenderness that I would like; but they do not stop me thinking ahead with delight to springtime in the lovely land of Italy.

But nothing has been done until the documents are signed. So this fine castle in the air might never materialise. Love me and write to me.

Tell everyone the pure and exact truth, which is that I have no credit. I'm receiving five to six requests per week, but I can't grant them – which creates at least one new enemy a month for me, i.e. twelve enemies per year, all saying that ever since M. Beyle has been this and that, he's so haughty no one dare address him, he refuses to recognise his old friends, etc., and other equally reasonable things.

To counterbalance this unfortunate effect, keep presenting compliments to everyone. Every time a letter from me arrives, say that it contains compliments and respects for everything you happen to come into contact with.

Paris, 8th April 1811

[…] For you: I still hope to spend two months in Rome. Chance events have prevented His Majesty from giving the orders for my departure. I wasn't too bothered at having to stay because of the list of auditeurs that was being drawn up. It's finally been completed and I'm in the first class. I'll be going to Rome filled with the sweetest emotions. I'll refrain from going to wallow in gloom in the rue de Bonne.[233] I expect to be travelling via Dijon, Lausanne, the Simplon. But if I could be sure of finding you at Thuellin, I'd call by. […]

HENRI

My dear friend, I have received from our good old grandfather a letter that's made me a bit worried about you. **This letter and chiefly the name of Albert in your last letter**[234] give me a strong desire to spend a few hours with you, or to receive a long letter in which you can tell me what you're feeling. Remember above all this great and immutable truth: all men are cold-hearted and mediocre and love to hurt anybody they think is happy.

People think you are happy. So you can expect a great deal of petty and vulgar spitefulness from the same people who smile at you. Whatever plan you make, remember my maxim. Write it on a window pane at Thuellin, with a diamond. This truth shows how little one must count on men, and will prevent you from suffering many disappointments. This truth cries out to us to seek happiness in our thoughts and our feelings. This, in my view, is the only place that people above the common run can find happiness. Someone like Clet, the chemist, will find it in earning a hundred *écus*, a woman of the same kind in wearing a certain hat; but you and I would seek for happiness in such things in vain. If we are so simple-minded as to chase after the happiness of petty souls, we will be astonished, once we reach the object of our quest, to find that they are happy and we are bored. It's perfectly simple: a fox needs chickens and a pig needs potatoes. We're not of the same species as those animals. The same food doesn't suit us.

Remember that those animals, thinking that you and I are happy, will always act in an envious way towards us. So let's make sure we don't give them any occasion to do so. I'm afraid you may behave in some impulsive way that may compromise **your future happyness**. Remember that it is necessary **to the happyness of a woman** to be esteemed, and that dressing up as a man and going for a stroll to the Bastille,[235] which would have proved someone to be a great soul, incapable of spite, in the view of a tribunal composed of Molière, Helvétius and Shakespeare, appears like a terrible misdeed to the inhabitants of the Grand-Rue. When will I see you? I passionately long to have you in Paris. Thanks to the slowness of **our father**, I have been neither to Petersburg, nor to Rome. If I had, I'd have stopped off to see you and maybe taken you off with me. **I will perhaps marry, but the heart is for nothing in this affair**. I despair of ever finding the character that I imagined **in** V[ictorine]. **I will marry a** nobody. But if **our father** continues to dither, it will all come to nothing. You really must be a man possessed not to do something for your son, and to stop other people doing anything too. It's an important lesson. What can one expect from other men if this is how a father behaves? I've sent a draft for a deed of gift; as if he didn't know how to dictate such a document to the first notary he finds. The notary here laughed as he drew up this draft; he told me that the least little village notary knew all this by heart. Fare-well, this thought is really hurtful. Since you and I are the only ones who know how to love in this family, let's love each other intensely. Come to Paris or write me a long letter. I've received the gloves. A thousand affectionate things to Périer and M. Allard when you pass through Voiron. Don't forget Mme Colomb and Mlle Edwige.

Milan, 10th September 1811

M. Z. has been so kind as to allow me to take some time off, and I have come to embrace my old friends and see Rome and Naples. Milan fills me with the most tender memories. I spent the sweet years of adolescence here. It is here that I have loved the most. It is here, too, that my character was shaped. I see every day that I have the heart of an Italian, minus the murders – anyway, it is unfair of people to accuse the Italians of these.

But this wild love for gaiety, music and a free-and-easy lifestyle, the art of getting on with the enjoyment of life, etc., all that is characteristic of your Milanese. You'll mock this tissue of nonsense, but it's just for you. I'll send my letter via Paris so that the postmark doesn't give away my whereabouts.

Burn my letter and don't tell anyone what's in it.

From 20th to 30th October, I'll go to embrace my grandfather *e tutti quanti*.[236] But I can sense that, on my way home from Italy, I'll find it very difficult to remain for more than twenty-four or thirty-six hours with those great souls.

I'd love to spend a few days with you at Thuellin; I'll pretend I'm ill.

Write to me, *poste restante, in Turin and Milan*. That makes two letters.

An insignificant letter can tell me which village I need to stop off in near Thuellin. I'll come via mail coach from Milan to Lyon and, passing through Thuellin, I'll set foot on the ground and walk one or two leagues, or borrow a peasant's horse.

From there I'll go to Grenoble and come back via Thuellin, where I'll go down with a fever for three or four days.

Make sure that the address of the letters you write to me doesn't betray my secret, since this would lead to me being deluged with questions.

Farewell, you know how much I love you. If only one day we could go on this lovely trip together!

Write to me in Rome. I'll find your letter on my way to or from Naples. This is my route, more or less:

15th, leave Milan; 21st, arrive in Rome; 25th in Naples; leave on 10th October; in Rome for six days; in Milan on 22nd October; in Thuellin from 26th to 30th; in Paris on 6th November.

Rome, 2nd October 1811

I'm well, and I'm filled with admiration. I've seen the *loggia* of Raphael and I've decided that you should sell your shirt to see them if you haven't done so, and to see them again if you've already admired them.

What touched me most about my trip to Italy is the birdsong in the Coliseum. Farewell; keep the trip secret, but give my news to our grandfather and to *tutti quanti*.

The appointment of M. le Duc de Feltre may prolong my stay in Milan. I'll be there on 25th October, staying for fifteen to twenty days.

I love you.

HENRY

Milan, 29th October 1811

[…] Ah, my dear, how I missed you in Italy! When by chance you have just a heart and a shirt, you need to sell your shirt to see the area around

Lago Maggiore, Santa Croce in Florence, the Vatican in Rome, and Vesuvius in Naples.[237] I know sixty *Voyages to Italy*; can you believe it – there are only two that are halfway decent? The most frigid of all is Lalande's,[238] and that's why I advise you to bring it if you ever come here. It's so glacial that it won't be able to spoil your sensations, and it indicates everything you should see; I think you still know Italian; I remember you'd got on really well with the language six years ago. Why, my dearest, do we have to be separated by such long intervals? But I hope this one will be the last of its kind. I'll probably be able to take leave every year. I hope I'll be able to take leave soon. I also hope you'll make your mind up to come and stay over in my fourth-floor apartment in the rue Neuve-du-Luxembourg. One has to see Paris so as not to be tormented by this great phantom. You'll discover the finest things in the world here; but it's a harem: everyone is a eunuch, even the master. Sublimity is dead; the inhabitants think of their petty vanities, their petty evening gatherings, the fate of some light comedy written by one of their friends, etc.

The peoples of Italy, on the contrary, are bilious, *not at all nice*; the rabble of Italy, indeed, are the most exasperating in the world, and unfortunately a traveller is always in contact with the rabble; the inns are the dirtiest in the world; however, after considerable effort, I found some very clean ones in Milan, Bologna, Florence, Rome and Naples; but you have to make sure you don't stop anywhere else; fortunately, all the cities are forty or fifty leagues apart.

If you make due allowance in advance for all these drawbacks, so as not to be irritated by them when you arrive, you will find a people born for the arts, in other words, excessively sensitive. An old notary of fifty-five, a more sordid old miser than M. Girard the chemist, will swoon quite sincerely in front of a Virgin by Correggio, will talk about it for twenty-four hours, will think of nothing else and, what is more, will spend ten *louis* on a copy. That same man, in the evening, at an opera by Simon Mayer, will shout himself hoarse yelling: *Ancora* (*encore!*). After these two sallies, he'll relapse into his avarice and his sordid ways.

Commonplace souls do however offer one observation: here, everything is done *naturally*; there are far fewer vanities. I often used to tempt the people of this country with a way of concealing the ridiculous things they indulge in; their reply always came down to this:

'Why should that bother me?'

If your tastes so incline you, you will increase the pleasures of your trip to Italy by reading beforehand the *Lives* of Michelangelo, Raphael, Correggio, Titian, Guido Reni, Domenichino, Leonardo da Vinci, Annibale Carracci.

With the lives of these eight men, who lived from 1460 to 1560, you'll know plenty. These *Lives* were written, along with many others, by a contemporary painter by the name of Vasari. You'll be able to follow his Italian, but his work is full of useless remarks. Will you have enough patience to devour him? Vasari must be in the library. Don't poison yourself with the stupid comments of one Cochin; instead, read the discourses of Sir Joshua Reynolds, the London painter. Some of them are translated in the first years of the *Bibliothèque britannique*.

As for music, if you're going to enjoy it here you need to know the *Matrimonio segreto* by heart; you can add *Figaro* or *Don Giovanni*, by the melancholy Mozart, and your heart will be prepared. If you want the history of music, ask in the library for **the History of music by Burney**, or **the Travel of Burney throught Italy in order of knowing the state of music**.[239]

Farewell, my hen's quill is wearying me and must be wearying you more than me. I laughed at the anger **of great father upon the new** cousin. I'm delighted to see you taking the platitudes of this world from their comic side. That's the right thing to do. Write me a reply. What is happening **in the heart of our father upon me and my title of** baron? I've almost stopped thinking about it.

Paris, 6th December 1811

A few words are better than nothing at all; I wish you'd keep remembering that. Imagine a man at a delightful ball, where all the women are attired with grace; the glow of pleasure gleams in their eyes, and you can spot when their gaze turns to their lovers. This fine place is adorned with great taste, with luxury and grandeur; a thousand candles shed a heavenly radiance; a sweet perfume in the air adds the final touch of ecstasy. The sensitive soul that finds itself in this place of delight, the highly-strung man, is forced to leave the ballroom; he finds outside a thick fog, a rainy night, and mud everywhere; he stumbles three or four times and finally falls into a ditch filled with dung.

That, in summary form, is the story of my return from Italy. In order to console myself for the physical and moral platitudes that I had to put up with en route, I imagined that charming little A, waiting for me with all her love, in my apartment, next to a roaring fire. I arrive: Madame left a good while ago. I passed the evening feeling like a rejected lover; I felt that my despair wasn't very sensible, but I was indeed desperate. The lovely little thing will be coming back on 18th December. […]

I caught a glimpse of Mlle V; just as my eyes fell on her, I looked fatuous and insolent; I was superb, particularly thanks to my plumed hat; I whipped up my horse with all possible majesty. She struck me as really pale, and I may have looked really fatuous to her. I was so taken aback I didn't greet her; I hope to do so the first fine day when people go out for a stroll through the Tuileries.

Farewell; come and see this part of the country. If you miss out this winter, I might never be able to show it to you. So use all your feminine wiles and as much masculine character as you can to come up to my fourth storey.

8th December 1811

You've asked me, dearest, to give you a thorough account of my trip to Italy; I don't really have the time.

In general, there are four things to observe in Italy:

The state of the soil or the climate;

The character of the inhabitants;

The painting, sculpture and architecture;

The music.

I found the state of the soil very well described by Arthur Young.[240] As for the local character, nobody has described it; you have to look for it in history; M. Sismondi, a pupil without genius of an excellent school, showed this character in the *History of the Republics of the Middle Ages*: sensitive, without vanity, ardent, vindictive, almost incapable of French wit properly speaking, that of Voltaire and Duclos.

As for music, I am waiting for a book on this topic to arrive from Naples; I'll translate a score of pages for you; you'll see that music is currently degenerating. The year 1778 is remarkable: Voltaire, Rousseau, Garrick all died; all the arts were, in France, in their last period of decadence; but on the other hand it was the finest moment that music has ever known: Pergolesi, Cimarosa and Jomelli turned out songs that were equalled by nobody except for Mozart, but only in the melancholy genre.

As for painting, I was lucky enough to become acquainted with one of the finest painters in Italy; he dictated the attached list to me, indicating by numbers the rank that he thinks each painter deserves.

I've realised that I knew much less Italian than I'd reckoned. To get back into the language, I've been translating (and abbreviating) the history of the Florence School, the first of the five noted in the table attached. If I have the patience to complete this boring work, I'll send it to you.

I don't know any French book on painting that's much good. Some people have mentioned a book by Félibien to me;[241] since it wouldn't teach me Italian, I won't read it and I don't think I'm missing out on much. You can get *The Lives of the Painters* by Vasari; it's an Italian work, full of the most gossipy stories. In spite of that, you may well find some enjoyment in the adventures of the great painters, namely: Michelangelo, Leonardo da Vinci, Raphael, Correggio, Titian, Annibale Carracci, Guido Reni, Domenichino and Guercino.

The friend who went to Rome with me and taught me to appreciate their masterpieces thinks that Raphael is the best; Correggio comes second, and Annibale Carracci third. The last of the great painters is Raphael Mengs; he was born in Saxony and died in Rome in 1779.

As you will notice, the two greatest artists of the XVIIIth century, Mozart and Mengs, are German.

PS – I dictated this letter to explain a few things to the clodhopper who wrote it, and who is unfortunately not so stupid as to fail to understand everything I am dictating, but doesn't have the intelligence to avoid mistakes. Come to Paris this winter, if you want to find me still here.

Ferocity towards me is increasing; maybe it will drive me away. I haven't yet fallen into the melancholy state of those in disgrace; that may come; one should never despair. Don't tell anyone about any of this. Really, try and come before the middle of January. Come, Madame, shake off your inertia; remember that you are twenty-five and, if you fall into the habit of putting things off, you'll reach an age when your heart has withered without having seen things that *one needs to feel*.

R.S.V.P.

Paris, 14th July 1812

I received your lovely letter, my dearest. It gave me an intense pleasure as you told me all about your thoughts. I'll reply at leisure. […]

I'm leaving Paris for Vilna a week next Thursday, i.e. 23rd July, I think.[242] M. le duc de Cadore and His Most Serene Highness have deigned to show me a perfect kindness in these circumstances. I only wish MM. the money-lenders would do as much. On the eve of such a considerable trip, I find myself with nine hundred francs. If you're in Grenoble, try to get **our father** to promise he'll send me a few francs. Apart from the need for money to buy horses on the banks of the Niemen, I have a debt to my tailor crying out to be paid: two thousand and ten francs. I've sent the account to my father.

That, my dearest, is the dark side of the picture. As for the rest, I'm content. There's never any really satisfying position in life. Nothing excessive can last long. Ignorance of this truth long prevented me from sensing the agreeable aspects of my position. I've been more sensible over the past two years.

For **six weeks** there had been a void **in my heart**. **A passion who lived in it**, **since two years** suddenly died around the 13th of last month, **by the sight of the mediocrity of the object**.

What is mediocre in any field fills me with an insuperable sense of disgust. I was a little unhappy at no longer being in love. This latest jolt will put me back in the saddle. If I can, on my return, **I will see again my dear Italy. It is my true country**. Not that I have an exorbitant love for one or other thing in particular there; but that country chimes in with my character. […]

ODILE WATIER

Saint-Cloud, 23rd July 1812

Chance, my dearest, has provided me with a good opportunity to write. I'm leaving this evening, at seven, for the banks of the Dvina; I've come here to pick up the orders of Her Majesty the Empress. This princess has just honoured me with a conversation of several minutes on the route that I need to take, the difficulties of the journey, and so on; on leaving Her Majesty's, I went to see His Majesty the King of Rome;[243] but he was asleep, and Mme la comtesse de Montesquiou has just told me that it would be impossible to see him before three o'clock; so I have two hours to wait. It's rather uncomfortable, in full uniform and lace. Fortunately, I remembered that my position as inspector would perhaps give me some credit in the palace. I introduced myself, and they opened a room that's not being lived in at the moment for me.

There's nowhere greener and more tranquil than this fine spot, Saint-Cloud.

Here's my itinerary for Vilna: I'll travel very fast, having a mail coach in advance as far as Königsberg; but the gentle effects of pillage are starting to make themselves felt there; things are twice as bad in Kovno; it's said that, in the neighbourhood, you can travel fifty leagues without coming across a living creature (I regard all that as greatly exaggerated; they're just rumours in Paris, i.e. the height of absurdity). The prince arch-chancellor told me yesterday that I should try to have better luck than one of my colleagues, who took twenty-eight days to get from Paris to Vilna. It's through those ravaged deserts that it's difficult to advance, especially with a poor little Viennese calash crushed under the weight of a thousand parcels; absolutely everybody has decided to send something for me to take.

By the way, Gaëtan wanted to come with me; I told him it was physically impossible for my calash to take more than myself and my servant. Thereupon, he wrote me an impertinent letter, accusing me of having offered to take him along. In these circumstances I'm like the man of honour described by La Bruyère: my character vouches for me; everybody knows I don't like bores – and for twenty days at a time…! It's the pendant to the letter in which his father called me a charlatan; nobody can be less of one, since I'll make it clear to them at the earliest opportunity that they can regard me as no longer existing for them.

I'm delighted you've bought Shakespeare; he's still the truest painter I know.

Farewell; if you don't come to Paris, go to Milan via the Simplon and the Borromean Islands and come back via Mont Cenis.

Eckartsberga,[244] *27th July 1812*

Yesterday evening, my dear friend, after seventy-two hours of travel, I found myself, two leagues further on from the gloomy town of Fulda, one hundred and seventy-one leagues away from Paris. German slowness has prevented me from travelling so fast today. I've just stopped, for the first time since Paris, in a little village that you won't know any more about when I tell you that it's called Ekatesberg, which means, it seems to me, the mountain of Hecate. It's next to the battle of Jena and twelve leagues further on is the stone marking the place where Gustavus Adolphus was killed at the battle of Lützen.

In Weimar you can sense the presence of a prince who is a friend to the arts,[245] but I was disappointed to see that here, as at Gotha, nature has done nothing; it's as dull as in Paris. The route from Kösen to Eisenach, on the other hand, is often attractive thanks to the lovely woods lining it. Passing through Weimar, I looked everywhere for the château of the Belvedere; you can imagine why I'm interested in it.[246] **Give me some news of mistres Vict[orine].**

Am I going to Russia for four months or for two years? I have no idea. What I sense clearly is that my contentment is situated in the lovely land

Che il mare circonda
E che parte l'Alpe e l'Apenin.[247]

There are two lines of Italian poetry prettily arranged! Farewell, my soup has arrived; give my very best wishes to everybody. Give my news to our good old grandfather.

HENRI

Moscow, 4th October 1812,
essendo di servizio presso l'intendante generale[248]
(Journal of 14th to 15th September 1812)

I left my general having supper in the Apraxin Palace. As we left and were taking our leave of M. Z. in the courtyard, we realised that, apart from the fire in the Chinese town, which had been burning for several hours, fire had broken out near us, too; we went to see. The flames were very hot. This expedition gave me toothache. We were good-natured enough to arrest a soldier who'd just given two bayonet thrusts to a man who'd been drinking beer; I went so far as to draw my sword; I was even on the point of running the scoundrel through. Bourgeois took him off to the Governor's, who had him set free.

We withdrew at one o'clock, after uttering a good number of commonplace remarks against fires, which did not produce much of an effect, at least as far as we could see. Once we were back in the courtyard of the Apraxin, we got them to try a pump. I went to bed, tormented by toothache. It appears that several of those gentlemen were kind enough to take alarm and to run off at around two and five o'clock. As for me, I woke at seven, had my coach loaded up and joined the queue with M. Daru's coaches.

These went along the boulevard, opposite the club. Here I found Mme B., who tried to throw herself at my feet; this was a perfectly ridiculous recognition scene. I noticed that there wasn't the shadow of anything natural in what Mme B. was saying, and this naturally made me icy. However, I did a great deal for her, taking her fat sister-in-law into my calash and inviting her to put her *drozhki* behind my coach. She told me that Mme Sainte-Albe had told her a great deal about me.

The fire was rapidly approaching the house we had left. Our coaches stayed put on the boulevard for five or six hours. Bored by this inactivity, I went to look at the fire and stopped for an hour or two at Joinville's place.[249] The furnishing of his house inspired one with remarkable feelings of luxury and pleasure; together with Gillet and Busche, we drank three bottles of wine that restored us to life.

Here I read a few lines from an English translation of *Virginie* which, in the midst of the general coarseness, restored something of my finer feelings.

I went to see the fire with Louis.[250] We saw a certain Savoye, a gunner on horseback, drunk, belabouring an officer of the Guard with the flat of his sword and hurling stupid insults at him. He was very much in the wrong, and was obliged in the end to beg his pardon. One of his comrades in the pillaging plunged down a street in flames, where he was probably roasted alive. I witnessed a new proof of the general lack of character among the French. Louis was amusing himself by calming this man down, to the profit of a Guards officer who would have made things awkward for him at the first display of rivalry; instead of treating this scene of disorder with all the contempt it deserved, he was exposing himself to the same insults. For my part, I was filled with admiration at the patience of the Guards officer; I'd have lashed out at Savoye's nose with my sabre, which might have led to difficulties with the colonel. The officer acted more wisely.

At three o'clock I returned to the column of our coaches and my glum colleagues. In the wooden houses nearby, a storeroom full of flour and another of oats had just been discovered; I told my servants to take some. They started rushing round, and seemed to be taking a great deal, but in fact picked up very little. That's how they behave, always and everywhere, in the army; it's rather irritating. However much you try not to give a damn, as they are forever pleading that they have nothing, you end up losing your temper, and it often fills my days with gloom. Actually, I lose my temper much less than another man, but I have the unfortunate habit of getting angry. I envy certain of my colleagues: I believe you could tell them they were useless buggers and they wouldn't really get angry; they raise their voices a little, that's all. They toss their heads, as the Comtesse Palfy[251] told me. 'They'd be really unhappy if they didn't,' she added. She's right; but how can you demonstrate such resignation when you have a sensitive soul?

At around half past three, Gillet and I went to visit the house of Count Peter Soltykoff; it seemed as if it might be a lodging worthy of His Excellency. We went to the Kremlin to alert him; we stopped off at the home of General Dumas, which looks out over the crossroads.

General Kirgener had said to Louis, in my presence, 'If I can be given four thousand men, I can promise to set up fire breaks within six hours, and stop the blaze'. I was struck by the remark. (I doubt it would have worked. Rostopchin[252] kept re-lighting the fires; if we'd stopped the fire on the right, it would have sprung up on the left, in twenty different places.)

We saw M. Daru coming from the Kremlin, together with that fine fellow Marigner; we took him to the Soltykoff residence, which was inspected from top to bottom. As M. Daru decided that there were some drawbacks to the Soltykoff residence, he was invited to go and look at some others near the club. We saw the club, decorated in the French style, majestic and closed. There's nothing of the kind quite like it in Paris. After the club, we saw the house next door, vast and superb; finally, a pretty house, a white square building, which we decided to occupy.

We were very tired, I more than anyone. Ever since Smolensk, I've felt quite sapped of strength, and I'd been childish enough to work up some interest in inspecting these different houses and running round from one to the other. Well, maybe not interest – but I *did* run around a lot.

So we finally settled into this house, which looked as if it was lived in by a wealthy man with a love of the arts. It was set out very comfortably, full of little statuettes and pictures. There were some fine books, in particular Buffon, Voltaire (he's all over the place here), and *La Galerie du Palais-Royal*.

Violent attacks of diarrhoea meant that everyone was worried about the lack of wine. We were given the excellent news that we could find some in the cellars of the fine club I mentioned. I persuaded old Billet to go there. We made our way in through a superb stables and a garden that would have been beautiful if the trees in this part of the world didn't strike me as being irredeemably scrubby.

We ordered our servants to dive into this cellar; they sent out a great quantity of inferior white wine, damask tablecloths, towels ditto, but very worn. We pillaged the material to make sheets.

A little M. J[oly] from the quartermaster general's, who had come to *pillage and plunder* like us, started to make a present to us of the things we were taking. He said he was commandeering the house for the quartermaster general, and used this as an opportunity to moralise; I put him gently in his place.

My servant was completely drunk; he piled into the coach tablecloths, wine, a violin he'd pillaged for himself, and hundreds of other things. We rustled up a snack with some wine, and shared it with two or three colleagues.

The servants were putting the house in order, the fire was some way away from us and embellishing the atmosphere, up to a great height, with a copper-coloured smoke; we were making the best of things and we were just about to draw breath, when M. Daru came back and told us we needed to leave. I rose to the challenge stoically, but it nearly killed me.

My coach was full, I told that wretched bore B. to get in, he was in a real funk – I gave him a seat out of pity and so as to repay to someone else the kindness shown me by Biliotti. He's the stupidest and most tedious spoiled child I've ever met.

Before leaving the house, I pillaged a volume of Voltaire, the one entitled *Facéties*.

François's coaches had still not arrived. It was only around seven o'clock that we finally set off. We met a furious M. Daru. We headed directly towards the fire, along part of the boulevard. Little by little, we advanced through the smoke, and it became difficult to breathe; finally we made our way between blazing houses. All of our enterprises are perilous only because of the absolute lack of order and prudence. Here, a considerable column of coaches was plunging between the flames in an attempt to escape them. This manoeuvre would have been sensible only if a kernel of the city had been encircled with fire. This wasn't at all the case; the fire had seized on one side of the city and everyone had to get out; but it wasn't necessary to cross the fire; you needed to go round it.

The impossibility of the thing stopped us in our tracks; we turned back. As I was absorbed by the great spectacle in front of me, I forgot for a moment that I'd ordered my coach to turn round before the others. I was exhausted, I was on foot because my coach was full of what my servants had pillaged and because the scaredy-cat was ensconced there. I thought my coach would be lost in the fire. François got the horses to gallop ahead for a few minutes. The coach hadn't been in any danger, but my servants, like everybody else's, were drunk and capable of going off to sleep in the middle of a blazing street.

On our way back, we found General Kirgener on the boulevard; I was very pleased with him that day. He urged boldness (that is, commonsense) on us, and showed us there were three or four ways out.

At around eleven o'clock we were following one of these roads and our path cut across a queue and started quarrelling with coachmen of the King of Naples. I then realised that we were following the *Tverskoi*, or Tver road. We emerged from the city that was lit up by the finest blaze imaginable, forming a huge pyramid that, like the prayers of the faithful, had its base on the earth and its summit in the sky. The moon hung over this atmosphere of flame and smoke. It was an impressive spectacle, but I would have needed to be alone or surrounded by men of intelligence to enjoy it. What has ruined the Russian campaign for me is the fact that I've waged it with men who would have sneered at the Coliseum and the sea of Naples.

We were heading down a superb road towards a mansion called the *Petrovski*, where His Majesty had gone to find lodgings. Crash! Right in the middle of the road, I saw, from my coach, where I had been kindly granted just enough space to squeeze in, M. Daru's calash teetering and finally falling into a ditch. The road was only eighty feet wide. Curses, fury; it was extremely difficult to right the coach again.

Finally we reached a bivouac; it was facing the city. We could clearly see the huge pyramid formed by the pianos and sofas of Moscow, that we could have so enjoyed if it hadn't been for the outbreak of pyromania. That fellow Rostopchin will be seen as a rogue or as a Roman; we need to wait and see how this action of his will be judged. Today, they found a notice hanging on one of Rostopchin's mansions; it says he has furnishings worth a million, I believe, etc., but that he's burning it all so the brigands can't get their hands on it. The fact is that his fine palace in Moscow hasn't been burned down.

Once we reached the bivouac, we had a supper of raw fish, some figs and some wine. Such was the end of this wearing day, on which we had been in a state of agitation from seven in the morning until eleven in the evening. The worst thing is that, at eleven o'clock, sitting down in my calash to get some sleep next to that bore B., sitting on bottles covered with personal effects and blankets, I found that I was drunk on that poor-quality white wine pillaged from the club.

Hand this rambling letter on to Félix, he can put it with the others. I at least need to do something useful with these tedious sufferings, by reminding myself of how they came about. I'm still really fed up with my companions in arms. Farewell, write to me, and don't forget to have fun; life is short.

Decipher, if you can be bothered, the attached rough draft; it's a letter to Mme Z. and, what's more, the exact truth. I'm surrounded by fools who get on my nerves. On reflection, I've reached the conclusion that this is the last time I go any distance from my goal, *la mia cara Italia*. We don't have any ink; I've just managed to make seventy-five drops, and my long letter has used them all up. Anyway, farewell; don't show anyone else the other letter. I'm more than ever sick of bores; deliver yourself from them as fast as you can. I am going, I think, to be sent to a position twenty or thirty leagues from Moscow. We're still fighting the Russians just now.

Madame,

I absolutely must take advantage of the kindly permission you have deigned to grant me, and not altogether lose the habit of talking to kindly people; those with whom I have been surrounded for the past three months can hardly be described as such. They're always talking about serious things; these should be kept as short as possible and stepped across as if they were burning coals: but not at all, they put an exorbitant dose of importance into them, and what could be said in ten minutes thus requires an entire hour.

This, Madame, is a great drawback, and we are reduced to having to see people of this kind. For example, I haven't had a chance to speak to a woman since leaving the village of Mariampol, in Prussia; it's a fate we all share. It's a heavy price to pay for the spectacle of a city burning in the middle of the night and raising a pyramid of fire a league and a half wide up into the sky.

In five days we have been driven out of five palaces; finally, to get some peace and quiet, on the fifth day we went to bivouac a league outside the city. On our way we experienced the drawbacks of grandeur. We turned with our seventeen coaches into a street that had not yet really caught fire; but the flames travelled more quickly than our horses, and once we were in the middle of the street, the flames of the two rows of houses filled our horses with alarm; sparks stung them, the smoke suffocated us and it was only with the greatest difficulty that we managed to turn round and escape.

I will not describe, Madame, horrors much more horrible than that. One thing alone filled me with sadness: it was, on 20th September, I think, on our return into Moscow; the spectacle of that charming city, one of the most beautiful temples of pleasure, changed into black and stinking ruins, through which a few wretched dogs were wandering, and some women searching for food.

This city was unknown in Europe: there were six to eight hundred palaces of a kind you will not find anywhere in Paris. Everything there was arranged purely for pleasure. Stucco decorations and the freshest colours, the finest furniture from England, the most elegant swing mirrors, charming beds, sofas in a thousand ingenious shapes. There was not a single bedroom in which you could not find seating of four or five different kinds, somewhere convenient to lean on, all well-arranged – and perfect comfort was combined with the most brilliant elegance.

It's quite simple: there were a thousand people here with an income of between five and fifteen hundred thousand pounds. In Vienna, all these people are serious all their lives long and dream of being awarded St Stephen's Cross. In Paris, they seek what they call a pleasant existence, in other words one that gives them all the enjoyments of vanity; their hearts wither and dry and they lose any sense for what others are feeling.

In London, they want to play a part in national life; here, under a despotic government, they are obliged to fall back on pleasure to pass the time.

I think, Madame, that the fortunate Bellisle is with you: tell him that we can do nothing about his auditeur's uniform until the Minister for War has written that he no longer needs his talents.

Could you be so kind, Madame, as to present my respects to M. le comte B. and to deign to remember from time to time my deepest devotion?

Vilna, 7th December 1812

I am well, my dearest. I have often thought of you during the long journey from Moscow to here, which lasted fifty days. I have lost everything and have only the clothes on my back. What is much nicer is the fact that I'm now thin. I've had many physical pains, no psychological pleasure; but it's all forgotten now and I am ready to re-embark on His Majesty's service.

Königsberg, 28th December 1812

At Molodechno, I think, thirty leagues from Vilna, on the road to Minsk, feeling frozen and on the point of collapse, I took the wise decision to travel ahead of the army. Together with M. Busche I travelled four leagues in three hours: we were lucky enough still to find three horses at the post. We set off and arrived in Vilna feeling pretty exhausted. We set off again on 7th or 8th and arrived at Gumbinnen, where our strength gradually returned; from there I came here, travelling a few leagues ahead of M. Daru.

Once here, we saw everybody arriving, except for Gaëtan. It seems he was ill before Vilna. Here, M. Daru told me that he'd found him feeling utterly demoralised in Vilna, weeping and missing his mother. M. Daru lent him some money, and then his last horse and his last pair of boots – a really noble action in these times of upheaval when a horse meant life or death. I've tried to clear up all these unhappy circumstances; everybody deplores the fate of the poor young man, but nobody can add anything to what was said to M. Daru by his servants who were the last to see Gaëtan a league away from Kovno. While all this was happening, I was five or six leagues ahead. Generals and commissaries in chief have perished on this march; it is highly unlikely that Gaëtan, who didn't have the resoluteness one might desire, has held out; he might possibly have been taken prisoner.

Farewell, my dearest; this is a very sad piece of news; don't so much as mention it. I think that M. Daru, who behaved very nobly, will be writing to father. I escaped by force of resolve; I have often seen, from close up, a total lack of strength, and death.

Very best wishes to your excellent husband. Please give me some news: for a month I haven't had a word from Cularo.[253]

Farewell, etc.

My dear friend,

I've had to come here against my will, but I'm having a better time than I expected. To remember a few things and learn something useful about the art of knowing the men of this year of mine 1813, my first desire is still to withdraw to Italy, far from the fools and the frigid souls who people the North. France was a charming country from 1715 to 1789. Since then, there has been no society, and the country's real nature – lively but frigid – appears in all its platitude. I'm fully expecting (as much as anyone can expect anything when there is little interest in granting it) that this campaign will win me the *Intendance* of Florence, which is worth 20,000 francs and that I'd prefer for the amenities of the place to a post as prefect, even though, if due form were to be observed, I have every right to the latter.

Read my diary page if it amuses you. Then send it to Faure who's happy to assemble my diary for 1813.

Very warmest wishes to François. Buy Grimm's correspondence,[254] it accurately depicts the corruption of the monarchy in 1780.

Paris, 1st April [1814]

I am very well; the day before yesterday there was a fine battle at Pantin and Montmartre; I saw that mountain being captured.[255]

Everyone behaved well, there wasn't the least disorder. The marshals accomplished marvels. I would like some news of you all. The whole family is well. I'm at home.

Paris, 14th May [1814]

You will see, my dear Pauline, in today's paper, **the total fall of my hope**. So it's time to move on. I'll be in Lyon in a month; then I'm going to Genoa and Rome. I have written an official letter to the bastard[256] to ask him for some land that brings in two thousand four hundred francs. I've written to Félix[257] to ask him if I couldn't give full power of attorney to M. Ennemond Hélie. I'm selling my furniture and my cabriolet. The money I get from this sale will pay for my journey and I can live off the rest for a few months. Then the money that M. Gagnon's going to pay.

The problem is getting the thirty-seven thousand francs – the local creditors – to hear reason. If you can, push the bastard to be a decent chap once in his life. […]

Make no secret of my wretched state. Pity will reduce the hatred based on envy, and perhaps make the bastard feel a bit ashamed; either way, I really hope I never see him again, nor Cularo either.

F. BRENIER

23rd May [1814]

I've received your welcome letter. It really makes things clear. I'm glad you have seen war. It's interesting. (We have to make the most of our misfortunes.) I am wrestling with the prospect of misfortune. I am going to be forced to eat into what M. Gagnon owes me, to sell off the house, to pay off my creditors and, within three years, to die of starvation. The bastard, angry at seeing me sell off the house, disinherits me and I'm a poor devil.

I'm sending you the third volume of Mme de Staël. I've foolishly lent the first two out. As soon as I get them back, you can have them. It's good to read in the provinces. In spite of being horribly overblown, there are some ideas there, especially on the lifestyle of the ladies of Germany. The third volume is far and away the worst. Kant believing in innate ideas and Mme de Staël refuting Elvezio[258] by mere phrase-mongering are as ridiculous as can be. Don't get stuck in a rut out there in the provinces. […]

I am still planning to retire to Milan or Naples. Six thousand francs are worth twelve in those happy climes. The sale of the house will bring in twenty-five or thirty thousand francs … … … … … …30 000 F

M. Gagnon owes … … … … … … … … … … …16 000 F

46 000 F

I owe thirty-seven thousand, leaving nine thousand francs to live off. How can I resolve this problem? That's the problem I'm fencing with. […]

F. MAISSEANO

Write to me often. Have the Austrian officers being paying court to you?

Very best to Mme Derville. She and I are almost in the same inextricable mess. With a bit of fortitude, we may get by, but when we can start to feel comfortable, we will no longer have hearts fresh to enjoy it.

A masterpiece has just come out, costing three francs ten *sous*. It's the book by Benjamin Constant.[259] It's one continual allusion to Bonaparte's government. Pages 102 to 107 are better than Montesquieu. Try and get this book from Lyon.

Paris, 26th May 1814

I see with pleasure that I am still susceptible to passion. I was just coming out of the Théâtre Français when I saw *The Barber of Seville*, played by Mlle Mars. I was next to a young Russian officer, an aide-de-camp of General Waïssikoff (or something of the sort). His general is the son of a famous favourite of Paul I. This nice officer would, if I had been a woman, have inspired me with the most violent passion, a love like that of Hermione. I could sense its first impulses stirring within me; I was already feeling shy. I didn't dare look at him as much as I would have liked. If I'd been a woman, I'd have followed him to the ends of the earth. What a difference there is between a Frenchman and my officer! The latter is so natural, so tender!

Politeness and civilisation raise all men to mediocrity, but spoil and diminish those who might be excellent. There's nothing more disagreeable and coarse than some fool of a foreign officer without culture. But also, in France, what officer can compare himself with mine for the combination of naturalness and grandeur! If a woman had made such an impression on me, I'd have spent the night trying to find her home. Alas, even the comtesse Simonetta[260] made such an impression on me only rarely. I think that the uncertainty of my fate is increasing my sensibility.

[Milan], 28th October 1814

[…] It's been pouring bucketfuls for four days, but they're playing *Don Giovanni* every evening with *la Falsa sposa*, a ballet of a magnificence that is quite unknown in France. For 8 *sous*, a good Milanese can amuse himself, his nose in the air when presented with superb pieces, from a quarter past seven until half past midnight.

As for me, I'm too preoccupied by the things I see; after two hours, I'm tired and I go to visit people in the theatre boxes. I'd like to have you and Mme Derville present at this remarkable spectacle; but all the magic of the thing comes from the gambling here. There are superb rooms adjacent to the theatre that are worth 200,000 francs per year to the entrepreneur.

They are so pious in Vienna that there is considerable anxiety here that gambling might be banned;[261] in which case, the Milanese can kiss their pleasures goodbye, since they live only to eat, to make love, and to go to the theatre. A little bit of politics, when a particular act of an opera isn't any good; then they stop listening and become absorbed in making conjectures. Yesterday evening they were conjecturing that the **King of Naples**[262] is refusing to give up his crown and that M. de B[ellegarde] is going to Bologna with his army, to take him in hand and bring him down a step from the throne of Naples to occupy instead that of the Grand Duchy of Berg where, they say, he is being sent;[263] a fat lot I care. [...]

You'll notice that my credit has diminished among the ladies of Milan ever since I can no longer offer them any cachou.[264] The little balls of cachou were famous and the women who liked me used to pick them out of the box with their tongues. Every evening, the remark was made twice, sometimes three times, that it was impossible to pick up the little balls with your fingers.

I had six boxes of Widow Derosne's cachou in my trunk: the money has gone and the little balls of cachou too. How can I repair the breach this has made in my credit? Well, you must ask Girerd to buy ten forty-*sous* boxes from Widow Derosne, carnation, cinnamon and jasmine, and to give them to the Bonafoux stagecoach, addressed to M. Planta in Turin. If that's a bother for him, forget it. Keep an exact account of the expenses made on my behalf. The bundle of the ten boxes will pay the Bonafoux stagecoach as if it weighed five pounds, so that, given its smallness, it doesn't get lost. Dear Girerd needs to be a kind fellow and slip it to the coach driver himself, in secret. This will be a bit of a perk for the driver who looks after it. [...]

21st March 1825

Meta parere meta danaro,[265] the Italians say. Dominique,[266] who can give you nothing but *pareri*, has not written to you. I am amazed at how spiteful Joséphine has been. You must have made her jealous. Since you have some obligations towards her, I advise you never to say anything really negative about her. I never mentioned the trip to Italy to her, since I didn't want any responsibility for such a headstrong person. I could say a few things about you being headstrong too. If I had any fortune, you could cross your arms and let yourself go as you did at M. Lorr….'s. You know that's not the case. Considering: 1st that the climate is the treasure of those suffering from ill health and lack of money; 2nd that neither you nor Dominique have the spirit of intrigue indispensable in Paris; 3rd that in the country of the blind, the one-eyed man is king; I advise you to settle down as a schoolmistress in some convent in Rome or Naples, paying, as a pledge of good behaviour, eighty *louis*. If ever fortune smiles on me, I will come and get you out. When you don't have much money, you need to work and not stand gaping at the moon. What would you do if you came to Paris? Your real work is to find work. Try to be a bit reasonable and to understand these three reasons.

Yours ever.

B.

1. Until the end of 1805, Stendhal used – as did his compatriots – the French revolutionary calendar.

AUTUMN: Vendémiaire (22nd September – 21st October) ('vintagey')
Brumaire (22nd October – 20th November) ('misty')
Frimaire (21st November – 20th December) ('frosty')

WINTER: Nivose (21st December – 19th January) ('snowy')
Pluviose (20th January – 18th February) ('rainy')
Ventose (19th February – 20th March) ('windy')

SPRING: Germinal (21st March – 19th April) ('seedtime')
Floréal (20th April – 19th May) ('flowery')
Prairial (20th May – 18th June) ('meadowy')

SUMMER: Messidor (19th June – 18th July) ('harvesty')
Thermidor (19th July – 17th August) ('warm')
Fructidor (18th August – 16th September) ('fruitful')

2. Stendhal writes 'sans cella' instead of 'sans cela' – a habitual mistake. It caused him some embarrassment when he made it, copying out a letter in his first job as a clerk in Pierre Daru's Ministry of War. But he sometimes gloried in his cavalier attitude to spelling and grammar (and Pierre Daru made similar mistakes.)

3. Stendhal was to be romantically involved with Adèle and her mother: he lodged with the family when first in Paris.

4. Chalvet, an ex-teacher from Stendhal's school, the École centrale, was assistant librarian in the town library. Jean-François de La Harpe (1739–1803) was a writer and critic: his *Course in Literature* ran to 18 volumes and was published in 1799.

5. By Voltaire.

6. I.e. week, in the revolutionary calendar.

7. The cathedral of Milan, which Stendhal here contrasts with the Panthéon in Paris. The Milan *Duomo* was still unfinished at this time, though construction had started in 1386; in 1805, Napoleon ordered the façade to be completed.

8. Saint-André, a church in Grenoble.

9. The old fort of Bard, in the Valle d'Aosta, was holding out against the French vanguard. It was later demolished on Napoleon's orders. Stendhal refers to this episode in his autobiographical *Life of Henry Brulard*, which inspired the opening pages of W. G. Sebald's novel *Vertigo*.

10. Claix, a town to the south of Grenoble, set against beautiful mountain scenery, was a family property where Stendhal spent much of his youth.

11. The Place Grenette, a big square in Grenoble in which Stendhal's beloved grandfather, Dr Henri Gagnon, lived.

12. Pierre Daru (1767–1829) was a French administrator (and Secretary for War) highly prized by Napoleon ('he works like an ox and is as brave as a lion', the Emperor was to say of him on Saint Helena). He accompanied Bonaparte on his Italian Campaign; he was Stendhal's cousin and played a large part in furthering his career. 'Daru' may also

refer to Pierre's younger brother, Martial, a close friend and (as a socialiser and womaniser) early role-model for Stendhal. He was also present during the Second Italian campaign.

13. The French occupied this fort in June 1800.

14. The Porte de France is a triumphal arch in Grenoble.

15. This is Saint Charles Borromeo, who was born in the castle of Arona (destroyed by Napoleon's troops). His statue, known as the *Sancarleone*, was completed in 1698.

16. Michael Friedrich Benedikt von Melas (1729–1806) was an Austrian general in charge of the troops facing Napoleon.

17. Marion was the servant of Dr Gagnon.

18. Caroline (Marie-Zénaïde Caroline) was Stendhal's 'other' sister, the one he didn't get on with.

19. Gaëtan Gagnon, Stendhal's cousin, the son of his uncle, the charming libertine Romain Gagnon, son of Henri Gagnon.

20. Francis II was the last Emperor of the Holy Roman Empire, which, with little legal authority, he abolished (1806) after Napoleon's victory over his troops at Austerlitz (1805). Francis had already founded the Austrian Empire in 1804, and continued to rule over it until his death in 1835: he established a strict censorship and a network of counter-revolutionary spies that was to cause Stendhal many difficulties in later life (Stendhal was expelled from Austrian territories as a suspected revolutionary *carbonaro* in 1821). It is his repressive regime that casts a shadow across the world depicted in *The Charterhouse of Parma*.

21. I.e. Coccaglio, a small town in Lombardy.

22. The battle of Cassano had been fought on April 27th, 1799. Alexander Vasilyevich Suvorov, the Russian general in command of the Russian and Austrian troops, had in fact defeated Moreau here, but was then forced to conduct a fine strategic retreat through the ice and snow of the Alps in 1799–1800.

23. On the southern outskirts of Grenoble.

24. The Montée de Chalemont is a steep slope leading up to the Church of Sainte Marie d'en Haut in Grenoble.

25. Montfleury is a hillside over the valley of the river Isère near Grenoble.

26. Mlle Lassaigne ran a small school in Grenoble.

27. The Abbé Claude Le Ragois (d. c. 1683) was a French pedagogue who composed a history of France and Rome that went into several impressions.

28. A cousin of Stendhal's.

29. Romain Colomb was another of Stendhal's cousins. (Some editions read 'Clet' for 'Colomb'.)

30. The French *philosophe* Étienne de Condillac (1715–80) was born in Grenoble, but Stendhal's interest in him stemmed from something more than local piety – a fascination for logic in all its guises, especially when (as in Condillac's work) logic was closely linked to psychology.

31. 'To be', 'to have'.

32. *L'homme des champs, ou les Géorgiques françaises* [*The Man of the Fields, or the French Georgics*] was published in 1800 by Jacques Delille (1738–1813). He translated (or 'imitated') Virgil's *Georgics*, as well as the *Aeneid* and *Paradise Lost*.

33. A verse epic by Voltaire, based on the life of Henri IV and focusing on the theme of religious tolerance.

34. This is the speech by Iphigénie in Racine's play of that name, beginning 'Mon père' and ending 'que je leur vais coûter' (not, as – according to his editors – Stendhal wrote, 'que je leur vais conter'). In this speech Iphigénie confronts her father Agamemnon who is preparing to sacrifice her. The choice of this passage, in which a noble daughter assumes greater moral stature than her tyrannical father, probably appealed to Stendhal and (as he no doubt hoped) to the sister he wanted to learn it.

35. These plays, full of heroes and heroics, are all on historical and mythical themes, with the exception of Molière's comedy.

36. This last line is taken from Boileau's *Art poétique*, canto 3, where Boileau recommends that his readers love Homer's writings with an 'amour sincère; / C'est avoir profité que de savoir s'y plaire'. – Stendhal later grew to dislike Racine passionately: he thought the dramatist was a toady who died of chagrin when Louis XIV didn't give him the recognition he craved.

37. A (very free) translation of the opening lines of André Chénier's elegy 'Ô nécessité dure! Ô pesant esclavage!', included here to show that the young Stendhal was not averse to Hamletic *taedium vitae*, or its poetic imitations. Chénier (1762–94) had been guillotined, a victim of the Terror.

38. Louis II, Prince of Bourbon-Condé and Duc d'Enghien, was one of the greatest French generals.

39. 'Ce récit sans horreur se peut-il écouter?' – Achille is speaking in Act III Scene 5 of *Iphigénie*.

40. Two ways of saying 'I had to go'.

41. 'Father, mother, stupidity'.

42. Pygmalion was the brother of Dido, according to Virgil's *Aeneid*, and his tale is told also in Fénelon's *Les Aventures de Télémaque* of 1699. He secretly killed Dido's husband Sychaeus out of greed for gold.

43. The story of Marcus Curtius is told by Livy. The chasm into which he plunged on horseback, dressed in full armour, closed behind him, leaving a mysterious hole in the Roman Forum.

44. The reason he went to the shore was apparently so that he could practise orating over the roar of the waves.

45. Louis de Boissy (1694–1758) wrote the comedy *L'Homme du Jour [The Man of the Day]*, and Charles-Albert Demoustier (1760–1801) wrote *Les Femmes*. Throughout these years in Paris, Stendhal was immersed in theatre and planning plays of his own.

46. Marie-Anne-Florence Bernardy-Nones, known as Mademoiselle Fleury (1766–1818) was a celebrated French actress who played at the Comédie-Française.

47. Louise-Françoise Contat (1760–1813) was also a famous actress, noted in particular for her roles as a soubrette (or, at other times, a coquette) in the comedies of Marivaux and Beaumarchais (she was the first Suzanne in *Le Mariage de Figaro*).

48. Jacques de Vaucanson (1709–1782) was a French engineer: his automaton, the 'Flute Player', together with his mechanical 'Digesting Duck' and other ingenious devices, are considered to be early examples of robots.

49. The story about Monrose spurring Molière, the son of the King's tapestry maker, into a career as an actor is told in almost exactly the same terms by Isaac Disraeli in his *Curiosities of Literature* of 1791.

50. Aristides (530–468 BC) was an Athenian statesman. He was 'ostracized' (sent into temporary exile) – the story goes that at least one of his fellow-citizens voted for this measure because he was tired of Aristides always being called 'The Just'.

51. Georges-Louis Leclerc, comte de Buffon (1707–88) was a polymath : a great naturalist, mathematician and cosmologist, and a fine writer.

52. Voltaire admired this, Racine's last play, in which the High Priest Joad incites the Israelites to rise up against Queen Athaliah, but he also considered it to be a 'masterpiece of fanaticism'.

53. In this philosophical study (1734) of the 'greatness and decline of the Romans', Montesquieu analyses the decline and fall of the Roman Empire in terms of natural and historical causes such as economic factors. It has been suggested (by, among others, Stendhal himself) that Stendhal aimed to feel like Rousseau and to write like Montesquieu – with sobriety and concision.

54. Portia (Latin Porcia) was the daughter of Cato the Younger and the wife of Brutus: on the suicide of the latter, she is said to have swallowed live coals to follow him into death.

55. César Chesneau Dumarsais (1676–1756) published his *Principes de grammaire* in 1769; he contributed articles on grammar and philosophy (including the article 'Philosophe') to the *Encyclopédie*.

56. *Les Femmes savantes*, Act IV, scene 3: a satire against pedantry and blue-stockings.

57. L'abbé René Aubert de Vertot (1655–1735) was a French historian whose history of Rome is noted for its drama and colour.

58. The strict Abbé Raillane was the man chosen by Stendhal's father to be his private tutor. Stendhal found him unbearable.

59. Joseph Jérôme Lefrançois de Lalande (1732–1807) was a celebrated astronomer.

60. This was the method used by Dumarsais.

61. Stendhal had been appointed Michaud's aide-de-camp in 1801; the General had commended the young soldier's bravery at the crossing of the Brenta and received him frequently in his house in Paris. Mlle Duchesnois (stage name of Joséphine Rafuin) was a celebrated *tragédienne* of whom Stendhal was a devotee.

62. Cleveland is the protagonist of Prévost's novel *Histoire de Cleveland, fils naturel de Cromwell, ou le Philosophe anglais*, published between 1732 and 1739.

63. Gaius Mucius Scaevola was a perhaps mythical Roman youth: when captured by Lars Porsenna of Clusium and condemned to be burned, he contemptuously thrust his right hand into the flames. Porsenna, struck by his bravery, freed him: now that his right hand was useless, he was given the admiring nickname 'Scaevola', or 'caggy-handed'.

64. Charles Rollin (1661–1741) wrote a history of Rome that was left unfinished at his death.

65. Jean-Jacques is Rousseau; Claude-Adrien Helvétius (1715–1771) the French materialist philosopher whose realistic (or cynical) view of human nature – the opposite of Rousseau's – also influenced Stendhal; Charles Pinot Duclos (1704–1172) was a French writer whose works show a keen eye for the society of his time.

66. Bernard Le Bouyer de Fontenelle (1657–1757) was a French writer and *philosophe* who questioned Providence and the supernatural in favour of a more scientific approach to history and society.

67. Frascati's was a well-known garden and ballroom, with tables for gaming: it lasted until 1836.

68. Lauzun, Matta, and Gramont were celebrated courtiers in the age of Louis XIV.

69. Epimenides of Knossos in Crete was the sixth-century BC seer and philosopher. He is said to have fallen asleep in a cave dedicated to Zeus, awaking fifty-seven years later having been granted the gift of prophecy. He is also supposed to have said 'Cretans, always liars', one form of the interesting paradox known as 'the liar paradox'.

70. These are all plays by Goldoni. Stendhal had already translated his play *Zelinda e Lindoro* in 1801.

71. La Rive was the stage name of Jean Mauduit (1747–1827), a celebrated contemporary actor.

72. I have mimicked Pauline's occasional spelling mistakes.

73. This seems to be a reply to the letter Pauline refers to in the opening lines of hers of 26th August (above).

74. Voreppe was the location of Stendhal's grandfather's country estate, a few miles from Grenoble.

75. The sister of one of Stendhal's classmates at the Ecole centrale; according to the family story, one of her ancestors may have been acquainted with St Bruno at the Grande-Chartreuse. She had fallen in love with Stendhal, and her secret passion may have contributed to her 'breakdown'.

76. Angela Pietragrua, born around 1777; Stendhal had met her in Milan in 1800, by which time she was married. He was too timid to declare his love for her. He later had a stormy relationship with her between 1811 and 1815, and when they separated he was driven to thoughts of suicide.

77. Saint-Preux is the tutor of Julie, with whom he falls in love, in Rousseau's *Julie ou La Nouvelle Héloïse*.

78. The name means 'Nettles Street'; this old street was next to the Louvre. There is something almost Baudelairean in this odd little anecdote.

79. Rousseau.

80. '[the sound] divinely soft and gentle of an instrument' (Italian).

81. The formula that so perplexed Rousseau is: $(a + b)^2 = a^2 + 2ab + b^2$. See Rousseau's *Confessions*, Book VI.

82. At this point Stendhal adds a little geometrical sketch to illustrate the formula.

83. Fortuné Mante was a friend of Stendhal's from their schooldays. It was with Mante that Stendhal went to Marseilles to try and make money out of banking.

84. This episode is recounted in the second of Rousseau's *Rêveries du promeneur solitaire*.

85. 'Ah! We will find pity if heaven is not barbaric.' Cimarosa's *Il Matrimonio segreto* was a work that Stendhal adored from the moment he first heard it, in the Teatro Nuovo, Novara, June 1800. (Emperor Leopold II had so enjoyed its premiere in 1792 that he ordered it to be performed all over again, after supper.)

86. Manon Roland (1754–1793) was at first an enthusiastic supporter of the French Revolution, but became increasingly critical of its excesses and was guillotined on Robespierre's orders.

87. This was Catherine II (the Great), whose accession to the throne came about only when her husband was murdered.

88. Princess Kurakin was a highly-placed member of Catherine's court.

89. Claude Carloman de Rulhière (1735–1791) wrote an account of Catherine's bloodstained accession that, by agreement with the Russian government, he published only after her death.

90. Of mankind and its stupidity.

91. An observation that recurs, in a slightly varied form, in *The Red and the Black*, chapter 24: Parisian boys have plenty of style when fifteen, but by the age of eighteen they have become 'common'.

92. In her letters, Pauline sometimes expressed an anxiety about being too personal and trivial in relating her everyday life.

93. Mme de Staël's *De l'influence des passions sur le bonheur* – a book which Stendhal goes on to praise, though he thought that its author claimed a sensibility which she did not in fact possess.

94. 'We' is Stendhal and his current mistress, Mélanie Guilbert, an actress who had come to try her luck in Marseille, where Stendhal had arrived on 25th July.

95. The cours Saint-André.

96. *Robine* is a southern French dialect term for a small canal.

97. Le Cheylas is a small town 30 km from Grenoble.

98. A veal stew.

99. Many of Stendhal's recent letters, indeed many of his letters *tout court*, were full of complaints about his father's refusal to give him all the financial help he required.

100. Mélanie Guilbert.

101. Presumably a poetry reading under the auspices of the Greek lyric poet Anacreon (born c. 570 BC).

102. Still Mélanie.

103. Mélanie's daughter by another man.

104. Later in the letter she quotes Chénier's 'Souvent, las d'être esclave et de boire la lie' – see n. 37 above.

105. Both are by Destutt de Tracey, who became one of Stendhal's favourite writers (like Condillac, he combined a love of logic with an interest in psychology): Stendhal had just discovered this author and was encouraging his sister to read him.

106. Here (though Stendhal had also read Locke) probably a nickname for his friend Fortuné Mante, a good linguist but *not a thinker*.

107. I.e. the Regency of the Duc d'Orléans during the minority of Louis XV (1715–23): a period of general merriment after the austerities that engloomed the last years of Louis XIV.

108. Stendhal regularly recommended the 'interlinear' method for learning languages and reading foreign literature. Chateaubriand's great translation of *Paradise Lost* mimics Milton's syntax to similar effect.

109. *The Lectern*, a mock-heroic poem (1683).

110. Stendhal won first prize in the 'belles lettres' competition at the École centrale in Grenoble: his prize was the translation of Homer by Paul Jérémie Bitaubé (1732–1808); Guillaume Dubois de Rochefort had produced a translation of the *Iliad* in 1766.

111. Charles William Ferdinand, Duke of Brunswick-Lüneburg (1735–1806) died of the wounds he had received at the battle of Jena-Auerstedt.

112. Jean was a family servant.

113. 'My love', in approximate or medieval German.

114. August Wilhelm Iffland (1759–1814) was a German actor and dramatist.

115. The *Moniteur universel*, founded in 1789, was by this time the official organ of the French Government.

116. A reference to the battle of Jena-Auerstedt, fought near Naumburg on October 14th 1806.

117. Claude Roberjot (1752–99) was sent by the French Convention with two colleagues on a mission to the Congress of Rastadt; when Austria broke off negotiations, he was attacked and murdered by Austrian hussars.

118. Jean-Pierre Frédéric Ancillon (1766–1837), a noted contemporary historian who was, despite his French ancestry, a Prussian who lived in Berlin.

119. Wilhelmine de Griesheim.

120. The Peace of Tilsit had been signed on 8th July 1807.

121. *Corinne, ou L'Italie,* a contemporary novel by Madame de Staël, much of which consists of a tour guide to Italy.

122. The Hercynian Forest is the Harz.

123. Publius Quinctilius Varus was slain by Germanic troops under Arminius in the Teutoberg Forest (9 AD); the defeat involved the loss of three Roman legions.

124. Salzdahlum (*sic*), the site of a seventeenth to eighteenth-century *Schloss*.

125. Victorine Mounier, sister of Stendhal's friend Édouard Mounier. Stendhal had fallen in love with her during a stay in Grenoble at the beginning of 1802.

126. Mélanie Guilbert.

127. Édouard Mounier, Stendhal's friend, who later became a French peer.

128. Martial Daru.

129. A hamlet on the outskirts of Claix.

130. At the end of this letter, Stendhal added a little sketch of this hunting scene. The whole scene is recorded (differently) in his book, the *Life of Henry Brulard*, chapter 32.

131. These are both operas by Cimarosa.

132. These were all men of letters, though the identity of Letemps is not known.

133. The *Journal historique ou Mémoires littéraires* of Charles Collé (1709–83), a *chansonnier* and dramatic writer, had just been published in three volumes (Paris, 1807). His tone was gay, but he also attacked his many enemies – Enlightenment *philosophes* as well as the French Academy, Rousseau as well as Voltaire.

134. Mounier.

135. Probably the Darus, Pierre and Martial, respectively.

136. South of Hamburg.

137. German *Stube*.

138. This was because of the blockade imposed by Napoleon to isolate the continent from Britain.

139. Stendhal had already (in 1805) fallen in love with Alexandrine Daru, his boss's wife.

140. Pauline sometimes disguised herself as a man.

141. The Abbé Prévost (1697–1763) left his monastery before a transfer to a less strict order had been properly effected: as a result he became a fugitive and exile for many years.

142. These are both comedies by Charles Collé.

143. Stendhal had already recommended Koch's *Tableau des révolutions de l'Europe* (published in 3 vols in 1807).

144. Voltaire's *Essay on Customs and Manners*, and Condorcet's *On the Progress of Enlightenment* (by which title Stendhal is probably alluding to the *Sketch for a historical tableau of the progress of the human mind*), were both panoramas of human history from a philosophical perspective.

145. The Aegidienkirche in Brunswick.

146. Pope Gregory VII, who excommunicated Henry IV, the Holy Roman Emperor (not Frederick): Henry was forced to beg his forgiveness at Canossa.

147. The day he left Paris for Germany.

148. Victorine Mounier.

149. Victorine had been living at the Mallein home.

150. 'Dear sister' (Italian).

151. Séraphie Gagnon, cordially loathed by Stendhal.

152. See note 14.

153. Adèle Rebuffel (see note 43).

154. Pauline had in fact got officially married, to Daniel-François Périer-Lagrange, only the day before, 25th May 1810.

155. Elisabeth Gagnon, Stendhal's beloved great-aunt (older sister of Dr Henri Gagnon), had died on 6th April 1808. She had inspired Stendhal with her haughty character, her handsome Italianate face and her 'espagnolisme'.

156. The King of Westphalia, Jérôme Bonaparte. His daughter was Princess Mathilde, the society hostess of the Second Empire who became a friend of Flaubert.

157. A famous actor of the day (though Stendhal was not happy with his performance as Beaumarchais's Figaro in June 1802).

158. 'It' – getting married, and all it entailed.

159. I.e. Curtius (see note 43).

160. Livia Bialowieska.

161. *Verfluchte Franzosen*: 'damned Frenchmen' (German).

162. In Molière's comedy *Sganarelle*.

163. It is not clear to whom this refers: possibly Amélie de Bézieux.

164. They were: at Abensberg on 20th April, and Eckmühl on 22nd April.

165. This, and the other towns mentioned in this letter, are all in Bavaria.

166. Now usually spelled Altötting.

167. Probably the work by John Moore (1729–1802), *A view of society and manners in France, Switzerland, and Germany: with anecdotes relating to some eminent characters*, first published in 1779.

168. 'Imperial' troops (German).

169. *Branntwein*, German for hard liquor or spirits.

170. Guido Reni.

171. Goldsmith, actually: his pastoral elegy 'The Deserted Village' was published in 1770.

172. Stendhal went to Eisenstadt as a member of a commission sent to offer the crown of an independent Hungary to Prince Miklós Ferdinánd Esterházy. The Prince refused, the Empire was saved.

173. An imperial palace outside Vienna.

174. Mödling is just south of Vienna: it has a twelfth-century charnel house.

175. The Schottenkirche (*sic*), in the centre of Vienna, was the scene of Haydn's funeral on 15th June 1809.

176. 'Deh vieni alla finestra', sung outside the window of Elvira's maid.

177. Mozart's score actually requires a mandolin (but these were not always available in war-torn Austria).

178. But which one is this? The next aria is Zerlina's tender 'Vedrai, carino': but *Don Giovanni* was often given in different versions with misplaced arias…

179. The opera by Jean-François Lesueur, based on the 1788 novel by Bernardin de Saint-Pierre.

180. In Vienna.

181. He did visit her in Ancona, but not until 1811.

182. Pauline's husband and sister-in-law.

183. Maybe Stendhal heard 'Oh ja, gnädiger Herr': 'indeed you may, Sir'. Or 'Oh ja, Herr, g'rade' – 'Oh yes, Sir, straightaway'.

184. An *Auditeur* in Napoleon's regime was an auditor of the Council of State, i.e. was attached to one of the fifty councillors of state as a secretary, a position that was much prized, especially by Stendhal.

185. Wilhelmine de Griesheim ('Mina', the 'Minette' mentioned in the letter of 30th April 1807), Charlotte Knabelhuber and Babet were all women Stendhal had courted.

186. A mysterious reference to the enigmatic character in Goethe's symbolic novel *Elective Affinities*.

187. Stendhal had enquired whether his sister had read Cabanis four years previously. Pierre Jean Georges Cabanis (1757–1808) was a physiologist; his *Rapports du physique et du moral de l'homme* (*Relations between the physical and moral aspects of man*) had been published in 1802.

188. In the sense of 'temperament': 'humeur de dartre' is here a physiological term.

189. This pseudonym is borrowed from French linguist, historian, musicologist and traveller writer Charles de Brosses (1709–77).

190. I.e. the baronetcy that Stendhal was desperate to obtain.

191. This letter is entirely in English in the original.

192. Vienna.

193. His Majesty (Napoleon) to Antwerp.

194. By 'Z.', here and hereafter, Stendhal usually means Pierre Daru (probably from Italian 'zio' = 'uncle'). Mme Z. is his wife.

195. Stendhalian Gallicism, or 'sensible' in the sense of 'sensibility', i.e. 'sensitive'. Thomas Gray did indeed write a Latin ode in the album at the Grande Chartreuse, in 1742.

196. Stendhal was visiting Sèvres, the celebrated china factory, under the aegis of Pierre Daru, who was Intendant General of the Imperial household and in charge of Sèvres and other imperial factories such as the Gobelins tapestries.

197. I.e the military marshals of the Empire appointed by Napoleon, such as Soult et al mentioned a few lines later.

198. Jean-Baptiste Isabey (1767–1855) was a celebrated painter and miniaturist, favoured by Napoleon and Joséphine.

199. Pierre Daru.

200. Escarbagnas, a comic character in Molière's *La Comtesse d'Escarbagnas*.

201. Stendhal was to be appointed Inspector General of the Imperial Crown Furniture in August of this year.

202. Tasso's *Gerusalemme liberata*: this canto is on the theme of 'gather ye rosebuds while ye may'.

203. Victorine Mounier.

204. Henri Beyle – Stendhal himself.

205. Julie de Lespinasse (1732–1776) lived, and died, for 'amour passion' and works of kindness.

206. Johanna Baillie (1762–1851) was a Scottish poet admired by Walter Scott.

207. Chamfort (1741–94) was a French aphorist ('Any man who reaches forty without being a misanthrope has never loved mankind') who died (after several weeks' suffering) as the result of an attempt at suicide undertaken while threatened by arrest during the latter days of the Terror.

208. His Majesty Napoleon.

209. The column had a statue of Napoleon on top (as does its more recent avatar).

210. Victorine Mounier.

211. Pauline's husband.

212. Mme de Staël's novel.

213. I.e. the 'name day' of Martial Daru.

214. This was a ball given to celebrate Napoleon's marriage to Maria Louisa.

215. Pierre Daru.

216. I.e. 'livres' – (French) pounds.

217. Then Prefect of the *département* of Corrèze.

218. Alphonse Périer, whom Stendhal called in one of his letters (in his English phraseology) 'cool english Alphonso' was to become *député* for Grenoble.

219. Expense, costs.

220. Félix Faure (not the later statesman) was one of Stendhal's more useful friends, both during the Napoleonic wars and as a legal advisor.

221. A writer to whose politics and 'overblown' style Stendhal was usually strongly averse.

222. 'La chasse au bonheur', one of Stendhal's most famous phrases.

223. Thomas Surr was an early nineteenth-century English writer.

224. Camille Périer, one of Pauline's in-laws.

225. Still harping on Victorine Mounier and 'his' (i.e. her) marriage.

226. Stendhal was still obsessed with getting a baronetcy.

227. Or Thuellin, the château outside Grenoble where Pauline and her husband lived.

228. A version of the story of Cinderella that was wildly popular.

229. Pépin de Bellisle – a close friend of Stendhal's.

230. Carlo Antonio Porporati (1741–1816) was an Italian artist, known in particular for his engravings.

231. Stendhal discovered the *Éléments d'idéologie* of Destutt de Tracy in 1805 and remained an ardent admirer of his attempt to treat morality and politics in a scientific way, tracing all ideas back to sensations.

232. The things seen.

233. Where his father was now living.

234. Pauline was having an affair with a man called Albert.

235. The fortress overlooking Grenoble.

236. 'And everyone' (Italian).

237. Stendhal had climbed Vesuvius earlier that year.

238. Joseph Jérôme Le Français de Lalande wrote a *Voyage en Italie* published in 1790.

239. Burney's preferred title, not quite as good as Stendhal's, was *The Present State of Music in France and Italy, or, The Journal of a Tour through those Countries, undertaken to collect materials for a General History of Music* (1771).

240. Arthur Young (1791–1820) was an English writer on economics and agronomy. He wrote an account of his 1789 trip to Italy.

241. André Félibien (1619–1715) wrote a series of *Entretiens* on the lives of painters.

242. As part of the Grande Armée as it set off to invade Russia.

243. Napoleon's son, born on March 20th, 1811.

244. A small town to the west of Naumburg.

245. Goethe's patron Karl August, Grand Duke of Saxe-Weimar-Eisenach.

246. Joseph Mounier, Victorine's father, had founded a school there.

247. 'Which the sea surrounds/and which the Alps and Apennines divide' – a loose reminiscence of Petrarch.

248. 'While on duty with the Intendant General' (Italian).

249. Louis de Joinville, an acquaintance of Stendhal's since 1801 in Milan.

250. The same.

251. Stendhal's nickname for Mme Daru.

252. Count Fyodor Vasilievich Rostopchin was the military governor of Moscow who instigated (or did nothing to stop) the fires that broke out there after Napoleon's entry.

253. Cularo was an ancient name for Grenoble. Stendhal liked using it because of its vulgar sound in French ('cul').

254. Friedrich Melchior, Baron von Grimm (1723–1807) had painted his contemporaries in a harsh light.

255. The Russians had taken Montmartre on 30th March. Stendhal had just arrived back in Paris, on 27th.

256. Stendhal's father.

257. Félix-Romain Gagnon, Stendhal's uncle (the 'M. Gagnon' of a few lines down).

258. I.e. Helvétius.

259. *De l'esprit de conquête et de l'usurpation, dans leurs rapports avec la civilisation européenne*, an anti-Napoleonic tract, had been published in Germany in January 1814 and appeared in Paris in April of that year.

260. Stendhal's nickname for Angelina Pietragrua.

261. It was indeed banned in Milan, in 1815.

262. Joachim Murat was Napoleon's appointee as King of Naples (and his brother-in-law), and was eventually captured and executed in 1815.

263. Napoleon had made him Grand Duke of Berg and Cleves in 1806.

264. A medicinal drug used rather like chewing-gum.

265. Half advice, half money.

266. Another name Stendhal gave himself. Joséphine, a few lines below, is Mme Bazire de Longueville who accompanied Pauline on her trip to Italy.

SOME DATES

1783   23rd January, Marie-Henri Beyle is born at 14, rue des Vieux-Jésuites, in Grenoble.

1786   His sister Pauline-Eléonore is born.

1790   23rd November, their mother dies in childbirth. In his autobiographical Vie de Henry Brulard, Stendhal claimed that his 'moral life' began at this point.

1791–95   S. is tutored by the tyrannical Abbé Raillane, 'a black-hearted rogue'. He later attends the new École centrale de Grenoble, where his penchant for wide reading is encouraged by several teachers (the authors introduced include Milton, Dryden, Hobbes, Locke, Helvétius, Condillac…).

1799   S. shares a first prize in mathematics. In October he leaves for Paris; he is disappointed in the city (no mountains nearby) and decides not to try the entrance exam for the École Polytechnique as he had planned. He becomes ill and depressed.

1800   S. lives with the Daru family in the Rue de Lille, Paris. Pierre Daru, his cousin, finds him a job in the Ministry of War.
May: he leaves for Italy, crossing the St Bernard Pass.
June: one evening in Novara, he first hears Cimarosa's *Il matrimonio segreto*.
20th June: he arrives in Milan. He is overjoyed to discover what he will often consider to be his true home. In the autumn he is appointed to the cavalry and the dragoons. His euphoria wears off under the monotony of garrison life in Italy.

1801   December, he obtains sick leave to return to Grenoble.

1802–05   Having handed in his resignation from the army, much to the dismay of Pierre Daru, S. works furiously in Paris, attempting to become a writer (a poet, a dramatist); he reads voraciously.

1805   January, he falls in love with the young actress Mélanie Guilbert whom he met at the end of 1804. He thinks of becoming a banker.

May–July: he follows Mélanie to Marseille, where she has made her début at the Grand-Théâtre. He works for Charles Meunier et Cie, importer of spices and colonial produce. Mélanie becomes his mistress.

1806   He gets bored with Mélanie. Pierre Daru is appointed Councillor of State and Intendant Général. S. conceives ideas of ambition and leaves Marseille for Paris.

16th October: he leaves for Germany, with Martial Daru.

29th October: he is sent to Brunswick as an assistant to the commissioners for war.

1807–08   Mainly in Brunswick, with trips to the Harz mountains, Hamburg, etc. His career in the imperial administration starts to take off.

1808   25th May, Pauline marries Daniel-François Périer-Lagrange. December: S. returns to Paris.

1809   S. is in Paris in the spring, then takes part in the Austrian campaign.

May–November: S. is in Vienna. He is put in charge of the military hospitals.

15th June: he attends the performance of Mozart's *Requiem* given in honour of Haydn (died 31st May).

October: Countess Alexandrine Daru, the wife of Pierre, arrives in Vienna. S. courts her.

1810   January: S. returns to Paris. Brilliant *mondain* life. Travels round the Paris region.

1st August: he is appointed auditeur to the War Department of the Council of State.

22nd August: appointed Inspecteur du Mobilier et des Bâtiments de la Couronne (in charge of the Emperor's furnishings and properties).

16th October: placed in charge of inventorying the Musée Napoléon (otherwise known as the Louvre).

16th December: he is presented to the Empress.

1811   January–April: unsuccessful vis-à-vis Alexandrine Daru, S. takes a singer, Angéline (or Angelina) Bereyter, as his mistress.

April–November: travels in Normandy and Italy. In Milan, Angela Pietragrua, whom he met during his first stay in Italy, finally becomes his mistress; he travels widely (Bologna, Florence, Rome, Naples, Ancona), working on a history of Italian painting that will be published in 1817.

1812   23rd July: he receives the order to accompany the Grande Armée into Russia.

September–October: in Moscow, where he sees the burning of the city. The French troops leave on 23rd October.

November: S. is put in charge of army supplies at Smolensk. He takes part in the retreat of the shattered Grande Armée back through Russia and Germany.

1813   end of January: he arrives back in Paris.

April–August: Campaign in Germany; S. in Sagan (Silesia) and Dresden.

September–November: on sick leave, S. goes to Milan and renews his affair with Angela Pietragrua.

1813–14   Winter: S. in Grenoble, organising the defence of the city.

1814   27th March–20th July: S. returns to Paris and witnesses the fall of the city to the Allies (31st March); decides to go abroad.

28th April: Napoleon abdicates: S., fearing ruin, works on his first book, *Vies de Haydn, de Mozart et de Métastase*.

10th August: he settles in Milan. Later this year he travels across northern Italy.

1815   He is still in Italy when he hears that Napoleon has escaped from Elba and landed in France. He decides to remain in Italy, and thus misses the battle of Waterloo (18th July) – he hears the news a week later. He continues work on his history of Italian painting.

1816   Mainly in Milan, S. frequents high society, meets Byron.

14th December: Pauline's husband dies, practically ruined, at the age of 40.

1817   April: S. visits Pauline in Grenoble.

He travels to Paris, London, Paris and Grenoble; then (21st November) onto Milan with Pauline. Their trip together is not a success, and they are never again as close as they had been.

This is the year in which 'Beyle' becomes 'Stendhal' – the signature he appends to *Rome, Naples et Florence en 1817*.

1818   March: he falls in love with Matilde (he calls her Métilde) Dembowksi, the greatest (unrequited) love of his life.

1819   20th June: his father dies, leaving nothing but debts. Stendhal is filled with unhappiness: his attempt to win Métilde is going nowhere. He travels in Florence, Milan, Grenoble, Paris, Milan…

1820–42 Lives in Italy and then Paris, writes *De l'Amour*, *Vie de Rossini*, *Racine et Shakspeare*, *Armance*, *Promenades dans Rome*, *Le Rouge et le Noir*, etc., is appointed consul at Civitavecchia near Rome, writes *La Chartreuse de Parme*, *Vie de Napoléon*, *Lamiel* (unfinished), *Lucien Leuwen* (unfinished), etc.

And Pauline?

She died in 1857, in near poverty, in Grenoble, having worked for a while as a spa attendant at Enghien-les-Bains. The person who looked after her in her final days was Stendhal's 'other' sister, the disliked, forgotten one: Caroline Zénaïde.

Stendhal was born Marie-Henri Beyle in Grenoble in 1783. He had an unhappy childhood, disliking both his father and the strict Jesuit atmosphere of their household, and so moved to Paris at the first opportunity. There his relatives found him a position at the Ministry of War, and in 1800 he entered Napoleon's army. He served both in Italy and in the failed Russian campaign of 1812. After Napoleon's downfall in 1814, Stendhal moved to Milan and it was here that he embarked upon his literary career.

He began publishing under the name Stendhal in 1817 with his travel book, *Rome, Naples et Florence en 1817*. This was better received in England than in his native France, and so he wrote a number of articles for British journals. By 1821 he was back in Paris and heavily involved with Countess Clementine Curial who sent him some 215 letters during their two-year affair. This relationship led to his work *De l'amour* [*On Love*] (1822), a psychological analysis of love. This was followed by *Armance* (1827), his first novel, and one very coolly received by critics.

His most famous work, *Le Rouge et le Noir* [*The Red and the Black*], appeared in 1831. A complex novel, this explored French society of the early nineteenth century, with the 'red' maybe symbolising the army, and the 'black' the church. His second masterpiece, *La Chartreuse de Parme* [*The Charterhouse of Parma*], was published in 1839, and was immediately praised by Balzac.

From 1841 Stendhal went on sick leave, and he died in March 1842, having suffered a fit in the street.

Stendhal and his work were regarded with some ambivalence by his contemporaries, but he has since come to be recognised as one of the originators of the modern novel, and is remembered today as a great figure of French literature.

Andrew Brown studied at the University of Cambridge, where he taught French for many years. He now works as a freelance teacher and translator, and is the author of *Roland Barthes: the Figures of Writing* (OUP, 1993). His translations for Hesperus include classic texts such as Zola's *For a Night of Love*, Voltaire's *Memoirs of the Life of Monsieur de Voltaire*, and Dumas's *The Corsican Brothers*, and works of contemporary fiction such as Laurent Gaudé's *The Scortas' Sun*, Yasmine Ghata's *The Calligraphers' Night* and Jacques-Pierre Amette's *Brecht's Lover*.